The
Hitch-Hiker's Guide to
DataEase

Gary Beard

SIGMA PRESS – Wilmslow, United Kingdom

First published in 1993 by

Sigma Press, 1 South Oak Lane, Wilmslow, Cheshire SK9 6AR, England.

Reprinted, 1994

British Library Cataloguing in Publication Data

A CIP catalogue record for this book is available from the British Library.

ISBN: 1-85058-505-9

Typesetting and design by

Sigma Press, Wilmslow

Printed in Malta by
Interprint Ltd.

Distributed by

John Wiley & Sons Ltd., Baffins Lane, Chichester, West Sussex, England.

CONTENTS

1

What is a Database?

I first encountered the word *database* while watching an episode of *Tomorrow's World* during the early eighties. For some reason the word stuck in my mind long enough after the TV programme for me to look up its definition in an encyclopedia:

DATABASE - A structured, centralised collection of data. Held by large organisations upon mainframes or minicomputers.

Even after reading the explanation twice I still wasn't much the wiser. However, as I came to understand computers a bit better, I started to realise the sort of problems the compilers of the encyclopedias had faced. They needed to provide a description, as concisely as possible, of a product whose characteristics and usage were so very wide ranging. In the circumstances, the thoroughness of their description has to be applauded. Fortunately this book has no such restrictions, so to business ... what is a database?

A database is essentially a place where information can be stored. Once there, that information becomes widely available for any number of purposes. Your local library could be considered to be a database - one that handles books. Only a few copies of any individual book, maybe only one, are actually owned by the library but any number of people can come into that library and use them. One piece of stored information available to lots of people, many times. In the computer world, a database program, such as DataEase, acts as the librarian, storing and retrieving data that you've placed upon a database.

Don't worry if it's still as clear as mud, I'll elucidate a bit further ....

A database handles information. Its first job is store away some data; its second, unsurprisingly, is to bring it back. The clever bit is that once the information has been filed away, it can then be used for lots of different things by people other than the person who supplied the original data.

If you are someone running a business this is a very big plus indeed. For as soon as something like a customer's name and address are entered into the database, those address details then become immediately available to your whole business: the advertising department, your sales office, your packaging section and, of course, most importantly, your billing people.

But that is not the only thing databases can turn their hand to. The information they are asked to hold is stored away very methodically, just as books in a library are placed upon shelves according to their subject and author's name. One of the benefits of this structured approach is that it enables data to be retrieved very quickly, and in a variety of ways. This allows the information to be utilised to the very maximum, which can bring about some unexpected results.

For example, banks were among the first institutions to start playing with databases. Not only did they have the big computers that were then required to run a database, but they also had the resources to finance such expensive projects. The data they stored, surprise, surprise, was financial details about their customers, and among the information collected was an item innocently named *Disposable income*. At the time it was just one of a number of statistics they liked to maintain, bankers being a breed of people who like playing with figures.

Then one day, a banker with an eye for business, realised that this sort of information could be used by people other than the bank, and what's more they would pay the bank handsomely to receive it. The people I am referring to are advertising agencies, the sort that make a habit of sending out half a forest of junk mail every year. Have you ever stopped to think how they know the people to target with their advertisements, and where they got the addresses from? The answer is, someone with a database.

Nowadays the Data Protection Act restricts the flow of such information, fears of Big Brother and all that, but there's still plenty of opportunity for a business to flourish from the information provided by its database.

Physical Structure

All right, so now we have some idea of what a database is, but how does it work?

A database holds information using things called *records, fields* and, of course, *data*. Ignoring the computer world for a moment, let's think of something nice, like that form you complete at the travel agent's when booking your summer holiday. It contains questions such as your destination, when you will be going and so on. Now that form could be called a record and its questions, fields. The information supplied in response to those questions will be the data. The data lives in fields which are in turn held upon records. Lots of records inhabit a database.

There are several types of database management systems around. They fall into three main categories: hierarchic, networked and relational. DataEase builds relational databases, which, in general, provide simpler and more versatile facilities than the other two formats.

The concept will become much clearer once you begin building the sample database described in this book.

Earlier it was mentioned how much care a database takes when putting away some data. One reason for this is that databases work by navigating from record to record. If information wasn't stored in a controlled manner, it could easily become lost. Records containing similar or related information can be linked using common fields known as *keys* or *key fields*. You could picture the internal organisation of a database to look something like a railway network map, with lots of linked records.

That is not to say that every record upon a database needs to be linked to every other. Data chains only form when required. Several such chains can exist quite happily within a database without inhibiting its ability to function efficiently.

Equally, there are occasions where solo records come into their own. They still have key fields that enable the database program to locate them but they perform no linking function. However, a database structure built entirely upon the concept of individualistic records would be very difficult and unwieldy to manipulate. So thought must be given right at the start of a project as to exactly what each record's role will be, what data each record is to contain and which fields are to be used as key fields.

Someone designing a database to handle airline passenger information might decide that three record forms are required. One will hold the passenger's name, address and flight information, another will store data concerning the plane and a third will hold details about luggage. Each of these records has to relate to the other for a complete picture of that customer's needs and requirements to be built up. However, each individual item of information about a passenger only needs to be recorded the once.

The database structure would be something like that shown on the next page.

You may notice that each Record contains a field named Pass No (it's to contain the passenger's reference number) while the rest of the record is made up of unique field names. This is the usual database arrangement, where one field acts as the Key field, providing the navigation link between database records. In this example there is only one such field, but there is no reason why a database could not be built with records containing two or three different key fields, each maybe acting as the link within a different chain arrangement.

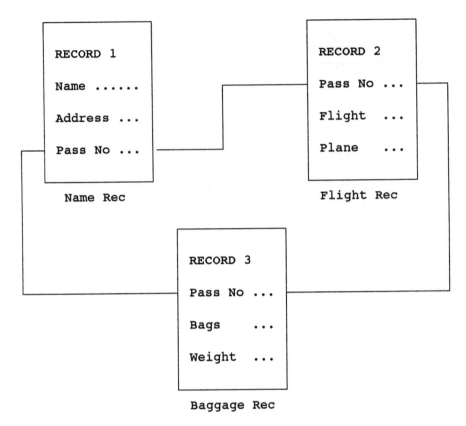

Baggage Rec

The airline passenger record structure

The passenger number contained in this special field, could have been automatically generated by the database or supplied by the booking clerk. It really does not matter, for, once a value for this key field has been calculated, it becomes possible to access any, or all, the other database records that contain the same value in their key fields. They can be retrieved in whatever combination or format is required. This type of structure provides a powerful set of data interrogation facilities.

Below, are example questions that might be asked of this database. Additionally, details are shown of the database processing required to provide the information.

How many people booked on a particular flight?
> Count the number of Flight records

What flight is a passenger named D. Ease booked on?
> Search for the name 'D Ease' on a Name record, in order to obtain the passenger's number. This can then be used as a key field value while searching for the associated Flight record upon which is stored the requested information.

Who do the bags labelled 5 and 6 belong to?

      Search for a Baggage record that has these bag numbers recorded upon it. It will also contain the passenger's number. Using this as the key value, locate the associated Name record upon which will be the passenger's name details.

Provide a list of all the passengers aboard flight number 51

      Search for a Flight record with a flight number of 51. Stored upon it will be a passenger's number. Use that number to link to a Name record and a passenger's name can be supplied. Repeat this processing until no more Record Type 2s can be found.

Because the data is only held in one place, should it ever require amendment, only a single updating action will be needed. Compare this against a situation where a passenger's flight details are repeated over a number of forms. Not only does this make the response to any of the above questions a major task but should it ever become necessary to move a passenger to another flight, each of those forms would require some amendment action. Even in the most efficient circumstances such a task would be difficult to implement fully within a short period of time. A database system, however, offers automatic, complete and consistent updating.

Databases in General

Although the word database is usually associated with computers, that does not mean electronic boxes provide their only habitat. The species is widely spread and can be found lurking around most offices. Take a closer look at that filing cabinet. It consists of three drawers. The top one has files recording people's names and addresses, the second contains folders with salary and pension information, while the third accommodates sales orders. That's a database - a manual system but still a fully functioning database for all that.

It satisfies all the identification criteria for a database described at the start of this chapter. The information pertaining to a business is held centrally, large organisations (and little ones for that matter) use one, data is filed away once, and anyone (providing they've got access to the keys) can use the information it contains.

A database running on a computer is the modern descendant of the one that inhabits a wooden cabinet. Being electronic it can be persuaded to hold more information and it is usually more efficient and quicker. However, these enhancements cannot be allowed to disguise the fact that it still shares exactly the same characteristics as its paper-based forebear. They both provide the same information and can be as easy to set up and maintain. So if you can handle a desk drawer, designing a computer database will not present a major challenge to you.

That really is the case. The electronic database requires no more planning and preparation than a filing cabinet. Sure, the giant databases running upon big business, Government and Local Authority mainframe computers are quite complex. They require specially trained acolytes to tend their needs and only cough up the goodies if asked politely. But the whole of their function could be replaced by a paper system that would achieve exactly the same results, albeit over a longer time period.

DataEase, the package used to construct the example database in this book, is as simple to use as its name suggests, while remaining a powerful information tool.

Database Information

Any database needs to reflect the view that information is a corporate asset. To achieve this, two perspectives need to be understood and accepted. Firstly, data belongs to the business or organisation as a whole, not just to the people who supplied the information. Secondly, if the information is to have any worth, it must be correct, accessible and unambiguous. A single comprehensive source of data will provide a sound basis upon which to base decision making.

Consider a business spread over two departments: the accounts office and a delivery unit. Each section has its own method of recording customers' names and addresses. The system works fine until a customer changes address. Now two separate sets of files need to be updated in order to record the new information. It only requires one file to be amended incorrectly, or even worse to be forgotten, and the entire system becomes corrupted. Either the product will be sent to the wrong address, or worse (at least from the accountant's point of view) the bill. In addition, it is a waste of expensive resources, to have to do the same job twice.

Were the customer details to have been held upon a database, and made available to both departments, the address amendment need have only been applied once. The new address details would then have become immediately available to BOTH sections of the business. This approach also alleviates the situation where only one section has been made aware of the address change. Communications within the non-database business would have to be excellent to prevent the obvious problem arising here.

Moreover, if two separate systems are in play, it is unlikely that the information will be recorded in exactly the same way. Thus it would be difficult for one section to exchange data with the other. Inconsistencies could also arise as each section concentrates on its own narrow business viewpoint. Neither will coincide with the correct view of the business, for example using different product codes for the same item.

Collecting data just once, and holding it in the same format, while allowing different people to share it, is a far more sensible approach. It also helps maintain data integrity. The means to do this is provided via a database.

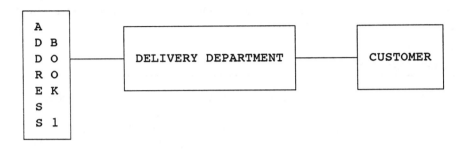

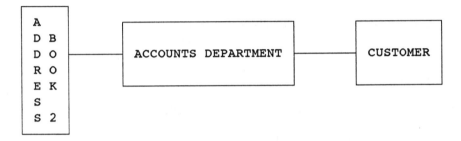

Systems designed in isolation

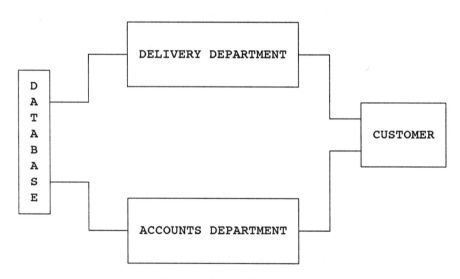

Systems sharing data

Now, as both departments have a common data source it is easier for the accounts department to confirm that the right orders have been addressed to the correct people, and for the delivery department to confirm payment have been received before shipping any goods out. Any last minute adjustments to an order would also be facilitated by this system.

Uses for Databases

The DVLC at Swansea owns a mammoth database holding information pertaining to tens of millions of vehicles. In contrast the secretary of a local fishing club also makes productive use of a database, albeit one only holding a few hundred records, in order to maintain details of the club's membership. In almost every business there is likely to be a situation where the case for constructing a database would be well founded.

How useful a database will be depends on a number of questions:

❏ Is work being repeated?

❏ Is the same information required by different people?

❏ Is there a need for data to be updated quickly and efficiently?

❏ Can the information be accessed easily?

The first three items on the list have already been covered by the examples provided in earlier sections. So let's discuss the last. This question is much broader than it might first appear. Most systems are able to answer straightforward questions efficiently; providing someone's name and address details, for example, is a simple enough task. But what about situations where the question is more complex?

For example, let us for a moment pretend that you own a photo development company. You've also got the Midas touch so over the years you've expanded the business from a single outlet to several branches spread around the Midlands. Each branch reports weekly to your head office such details as turnover, stock levels and customer account data. This data is stored upon a computer but not upon a database.

An accountants report has caused concern because of the amount of licence money being paid to a credit card company. You wish to determine, as quickly as possible, the volume of business your customer's conduct using that particular company's piece of plastic. In addition, you need to know which of your outlets handles that card most frequently and to what value. Any additional information would also be welcome, aiding your deliberations regarding limiting or abandoning your business policy of accepting payment through that credit card.

Well, fortunately this type of question is not one that is likely to occur often, but when it does an answer is required quickly.

Now, because most computer systems are only set up to handle every-day tasks, you would be most fortunate to have your non-database system geared up to respond promptly to that type of question. So what happens? A meaningful answer takes, maybe, a couple of weeks to produce, time which costs you money.

The information provided weekly by your branches was sufficient on which to base a response. But because it was fragmented and not contained in any one place, it took time to collate and analyse. Had the information been held upon a database, answers could have been provided the same day the original query was posed.

The nice thing about databases is that once the information has been filed away properly, it is a fairly straightforward process to retrieve it again. Well, usually anyway ... a database can be a warm friendly entity, bursting with the ability to furnish you with all the information it contains. Equally it can be a dour, intransigent concoction that has to be wooed carefully before it can be persuaded to part with its jealously hoarded data. The secret lies in how well a database has been planned and constructed.

Through the pages of this book my intention is to introduce you gently to the art of constructing simple databases. We will be using the DataEase package produced by DataEase International.

The Porterhouse Database

The database we are going to design together using DataEase is one that might be used by a University or College. To that end, it has been named Porterhouse.

The object of the database is to provide statistical information regarding the number of students attending the college, the courses they attend and details of the lecturers conducting such lessons.

It will also be able to identify the optimum means by which the college advertised itself. Address details of people using the colleges facilities are also maintained, plus some relevant data about them as individuals and their background. This will allow the college to determine what type of people it is attracting, and also, just as importantly, the people to whom its profile might be profitably heightened.

While its content, admittedly probably only appeals to harassed school headmasters, the database structure can, with only a minor amount of tinkering, be adjusted to serve other interests. Once you've completed this book such tinkering should be well within your scope.

2

Database Design

This is the point in the book from which it becomes DataEase specific. There's nothing like hands-on experience for learning a subject. So it might be a good idea if you can have a copy of the database software up and running on your PC before continuing any further. Should this not be possible, don't worry . . . but to misquote an old line: "A screen is better than a thousand words".

Upon entering DataEase you will be presented with a sign on screen that controls access to all the databases you will set up. On the right-hand side is a column within which are listed the names of all the databases so far built. Not surprisingly at this stage it only contains the text *0 NONE*. But were other databases to be present their titles would be displayed, each accompanied by a unique reference number.

These numbers are used by DataEase to make life easy for us humans. Instead of having to type in the name of a database and possibly misspelling it, all that is needed is to key the appropriate number. The database name will then be highlighted, while DataEase patiently waits for <Enter> to be pressed confirming the selection made. This friendly approach is used throughout DataEase whenever a decision regarding a choice of action needs to be made.

As option 0 is already highlighted all that is required at this stage is to press <Enter>. The program now wants to know the name of the database that you wish to be introduced. In this case we are intending to build a database named Porterhouse, so that has to be typed before <Enter> is once more pressed. Notice how the action of pressing <Enter> informs DataEase that all the information has been entered and that we are now ready to go on to the next job.

DataEase checks that a database does not already exist with the title provided. If it does the program will assume that access to it is required and will take steps to make it available. This process can be stopped quite easily by the pressing the <Esc> key which is on the top left-hand corner of your keyboard.

In common with most other PC software DataEase responds to <Esc> being pressing by cancelling the current action and returning to whatever it was doing before. In this situation the effect is more dramatic. Because the program is at its start point it will think that it is no longer required and will ask you if you really want to exit. An answer of No will easily re-start the program but its probably better to take care over the database name in the first instance.

Assuming that no other database named Porterhouse already exists, the program will continue by displaying the message:

Database does not exist in specified directory – Create a new database (y/n)?

A response of No, achieved by pressing the <N> key, will result in the prompt for a database name being repeated. On the other hand, the reward for making a positive reply, i.e by pressing the <Y> key, will be the creation of a new database named Porterhouse.

A message will next be displayed showing the letter that will be used to identify uniquely the new database files from those held for other databases. If you feel like playing around with DOS in order to maintain your database files this information will be useful, the files being labelled *USERkAAA.DBM, MENUkAAA.DBM* etc. where *k* is the key letter displayed. You can ignore this information as DataEase provides the full facilities for you to add, delete and back-up data without the need for you to acquire any DOS knowledge at all.

```
  D A T A E A S E  - S I G N   O N

 Directory: C:\DEASE\

 What is the database name?: PORTERHOUSE

 What is your name              :
```

The DataEase logging on screen

Below that message you will be prompted to supply your name. Now it's going to sound a bit silly when I say remember your own name, but whatever name you key in at this point will be the name DataEase recognises as the owner of the database. It will expect you to use the same name every time you want to use this particular database. Fail to use the exact same spelling or wording and DataEase will be unable to recognise you. So the name you use is important!

This database/name matching routine is the first stage of DataEase's data security procedures. The second involves the use of a password, which is the next item you will be requested to supply.

The best passwords are usually constructed out of a mixture of letters and numbers, examples being a car's registration number or a postcode, but these can be hard to remember or too obvious. The same rules applying to names. A recent password survey found that words such as *Help, Test, Fred, System* and even *Password* were in common use, so there's plenty of scope for originality. Puzzled by *Fred?* . . . have a look how close together those letters are on the keyboard.

The most important consideration, though, is that you can remember your security codes without recourse to writing them down. DataEase allows you up to three attempts to get the Name/Password combination correct before pulling the plug and evicting you from the program.

Having satisfied itself of your credentials DataEase next displays the main menu screen. This contains seven options from which you are invited to make a choice. Earlier when discussing the database name I made mention of how user friendly DataEase is with regard to menu decisions. This menu further emphasis that point, requiring only the menu option number to be pressed before it will provide the required processing.

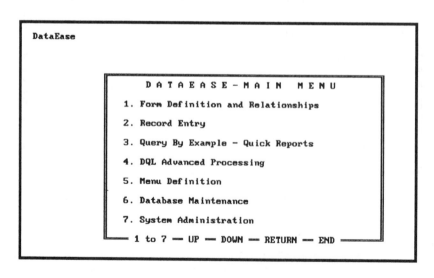

The DataEase Main Menu screen

Each option will be discussed in depth as it is accessed but here's a brief overview.

Form Definition and Relationships
Before any data can be stored upon a database its record structure needs to be described and any inter record relationships defined. This menu option provides the facilities to do this.

Record Entry
There are two methods of storing data upon a DataEase database. The one most new users of the program employ first is accessed via this menu option.

Query by Example – Quick Reports
As with data entry there are two methods of data retrieval. This menu option is the one that provides quick and simple data access.

DQL Advanced Processing
Don't be put off by the word *Advanced*. Yes, a firm knowledge of DataEase's vocabulary will stand you in good stead when using the facilities available within this menu option, but it is by no means a prerequisite. It allows more detailed information to be provided from the database and furnishes another means of recording data.

Menu Definition
It is possible to set up your own menu system containing procedures you have written yourself. Such systems, in effect, make the inner workings of DataEase invisible, thus allowing people with no computer knowledge to use the database.

Database Maintenance
This menu option provides the means to back-up data etc. It also allows DOS to be called without leaving the database.

System Administration
The final option provided by this menu allows you to manage other people's access to the database.

Form Definition

At this point in the construction of our new database we have yet to define the record structures. Until this has been done little else can take place so we've no option but to follow the path of least resistance and select the processing offered by menu option 1. This is done by pressing the number 1 on the keyboard and in return DataEase presents us with another menu display:

```
 Forms

   ┌────────────────────────────────────────────┐
   │  F O R M   D E F I N I T I O N   M E N U    │
   │  1. Define a Form                           │
   │  2. View or Modify a Form                   │
   │  3. Define Relationships                    │
   │  4. Delete a Form                           │
   │  5. Reorganize a Form                       │
   └── 1 to 5 ── UP ── DOWN ── RETURN ── END ────┘

   ┌────────────────────────────────────────────────────┐
   │  Please enter the form name to be defined : COURSE  │
   │                                                     │
   │                                                     │
   └────────────────────────────────────────────────────┘
```

The Form Definition Menu screen

This time only five choices are on offer:

Define a Form

View or Modify a Form

Define Relationships

Delete a Form

Reorganize a Form

The word *Form* is popular in that list, so what is a Form?. Simply it's a DataEase term for a record. In Chapter 1, records were discussed, with a travel agent's holiday booking form being cited as an example. DataEase just uses the word Form in place of Record. The two words are totally interchangeable within DataEase, so use whichever term you are happiest with, but for the sake of continuity this book will continue to refer to the items upon which information is stored as Forms.

Now, before diving in and defining a Form it's best to take a few moments out with a piece of paper and a pencil to consider exactly what information you wish the database to provide. This can be a fairly straightforward task when databases are as simple as the example being built within these pages. But more complex databases will benefit from careful thought being applied at this stage. Hastily constructed databases usually result in a great deal of reworking when it's discovered that a vital piece of data has been forgotten. Murphy's law usually means that such errors are not discovered until late in the project!

A number of aspects need to be considered at this point. The question to be asked is: What information is the database to provide? rather than: What information is it to hold? This reverse engineering type of approach helps to ensure that no important data is missed out or forgotten.

A housewife writing a shopping list first thinks of the meals she is going to provide for her family and then adds the necessary ingredients to her list. This is exactly the methodology being advised here.

So what goes on the shopping list first? The Dean of our fictional College requires this information before planning next year's college curriculum.

1: How many students are attending the college?

2: Who are they and where do they live?

3: What courses are they taking?

4: Which lecturers are holding those courses?

5: Which courses are most popular and which are not?

6: How were people attracted to the college?

7: What type of people are they?

8: How many lecturers does the college employ?

9: What are their names and addresses and how much are they paid?

10: What is the college's income?

Having decided what *outputs* are wanted from the database the Dean is now in a better position to establish what *inputs* are necessary, these being computerspeak for data entered on to the database.

An analysis of the questions raised above reveals that there are three broad output classes. Accordingly the questions within each class could be split up into separate columns under the headings Student, Lecturer and Course. Let's see how that works out:

Student	1, 2, 3, 4, 5, 6, 7 and 10
Lecturer	4, 8 and 9
Course	3, 4, 5 and 10

You may have noticed that some questions fall under more than one heading. This indicates a *Relationship*. For example Question 3 – What courses are they taking? –

requires two key pieces of information, namely a student's identity and a course title, hence its appearance against both headings. Indications of such relationships will be very helpful when the time comes to cover option 3, *Define a Relationship*, later in this chapter.

Having grouped the questions under separate headings it is now easy to decide what Forms need to be designed by simply replacing the word *Heading* with *Form*.

The next step is to determine what *Fields* are required on each form. Remember Field is the term used to describe pieces of information held upon a Form. To do this its necessary to examine each question closely and decide what information is needed to provide its answer.

1: How many students are attending the college?

DataEase loves counting and is able to provide a great deal of statistical information, particularly with regard to the number of forms it holds. Therefore, all that is required here is to ask DataEase to count the number of student forms it has. This makes life easy as there is no need to set up a field that specifically answers this question on any form.

2: Who are they and where do they live?

Some fields will be required to furnish answers to this query. Fortunately their titles are fairly obvious: Name, Address, etc. Even so they need to be written down in case they are forgotten. But before doing so, some other elements need to be considered. The prime two are the size (length) of a field and its characteristics . . . Is it a number or will it be text? The other factors will be covered as they arise.

Name

It is usual to split a person's name into three components: Surname, Christian names and Title. These will provide three field titles, each of which will obviously be text, thus answering one of the points to be considered. This leaves the field sizes to be determined.

Surname   Enough space should be allowed to cater for a few of the more exotic surnames floating around the average telephone directory. The example database has this field set up with 12 characters.

Christian names Sufficient room for two names should be provided – suggest 14 characters.

Title   There are not many titles flying around today other than perhaps a
            few Sirs (and of course Ladys). In fact, the choice is so limited that
            it would be nice to provide just a list of suggested titles, a sort of
            menu in fact. Fortunately the programmers behind DataEase thought
            the same and this facility has been provided. So all that's required is
            to work out the title list – say Mr, Mrs, Miss, Ms, Dr, Sir and Lady.

Address

Most printed forms contain the address within four lines. The usual line length is 20
characters and, of course, the characteristic, or format, is text. Additional lines are
added to hold data such as Postcodes and Telephone numbers so these should be
considered as well.

Postcode   It appears nationally that postcodes can be up to eight characters
            long and are made up of a mixture of numbers and text. Where such
            format mixtures arise DataEase requires you to describe the field as
            being text.

Telephone   Telephone numbers consist of an Area Code followed by a phone
            number. DataEase has as one of its field descriptions *phone no*.
            Unfortunately this is held in the American format so it's unsuitable
            for our purposes. Despair not, there is a way around the problem
            and this will be explained later. It is sufficient at this point to just
            record the need for this field.

It's probably going to be useful to record a person's work address details as well, so
this should also be noted with the same field description criteria.

3: What courses are they taking?

This question requires a number of fields in order to be fully answered.

Student number The fields to carry the names of people attending the college have
                already been allocated. However, it would be wearisome, and cause
                a lot of mistakes, if every time a student's details were recorded it
                was necessary to key in the full name. It would be much simpler,
                and more efficient, to take a leaf out of DataEase's book and just
                supply a reference code that's been uniquely associated with a
                particular student. Accordingly this will be a numeric field of four
                digits in size.

Course   The name or title of a course would also be useful. This will be a
                text field of 25 letters.

Course number   A similar case arises with the new Course field as with the name
                fields. Typing in a 25 character name every time it's referred to
                could become painful. So let's give it the same medication and
                allocate it an unique reference number, too. As there's not likely to
                be as many course subjects as students this field need only be three
                digits in length.

4: Which lecturers are holding these courses?

This question requires details of lecturers' identities to be linked against course
subjects. Fields already constructed provide most of the answers here. Lecturers'
name details can be held in fields identical to those planned to record student name
details, except, of course, there's no need to include any work address details. The
course information used to provide the answer to question 3 can also be usefully
applied to furnish information to this question.

5: Which courses are most popular and which are not?

On the face of it this is just another counting exercise for DataEase. But is it? Does
the person posing the question want to know which courses attracted the most
students or which classes were the best in terms of lecturer/student ratios?

In order to cover both answers, and a range in between, it will be necessary to plan
some more course information fields relating to student attendance.

Optimum   A two-digit number recording the optimum number of students for a
               class.

Maximum   Two digits required to measure a class's maximum population.

Minimum   The lowest number of students required to make a course viable.
               Again two digits in size.

Actual   Finally a double-digit field is needed to hold the actual class size.

6: How were people attracted to the college?

A choice field listing a selection of the ways the college advertises itself would help
to answer this question, plus of course getting DataEase to do a bit of maths. What
options should be provided? These basic choices should be sufficient: Word of
Mouth, Local Paper, Mailshot, Radio Advert and as a catch all, Other.

7: What type of people are they?

The answer to this question will serve many purposes. The prime one will be the
identification of the population groups to whom the college has most appeal. Such
data can be very useful, for example, when determining which areas of the populous

it would be most profitable to target as recipients of information concerning the college and its activities. Just as useful would be the negative report, namely the people it was failing to attract A couple of fields will be needed to supply this sort of information:

Age   This can be a sensitive question to ask of someone. So perhaps it would tactful to allow it to be answered in fairly vague, but defined, terms. This can be achieved best by making it another choice field that contains age ranges rather than a person's individual age. The usual settings applied in such situations are 18+, 21+ 30+, 40+ and 55+.

Employment   Again an imprecise answer will suffice for this question as it's groups of people, rather than an individual, the question's interested in. Thus another choice field can be used with this selection of employment options: Self Employed, Business, Student, Unemployed, Other.

Date enrolled   This field will record how long a student has been with the college – a good indication of how stable its customer base is. DataEase has a predefined format for fields such as this that is simply called Date.

8: How many lecturers does the college employ?

This is another counting exercise for DataEase. All that is required is a total of the number of Lecturer records held so no special fields need to be set up.

9: What are their names and addresses and how much are they paid?

As decided in response to Question 4, details relating to lecturers can be held in fields similar in construction to those planned to hold student address information. However, some additional fields are required.

Age   This needs to be recorded precisely for pension purposes so a choice field as set in Question 7 would be unsuitable. Accordingly the need for a two-digit (there's not too many centurion professors about) field needs to be noted.

Previous post   It's usual for employers to hold some historical data about the people they employ. A text field of 15 characters should be sufficient for this purpose.

Salary   A field is required that holds the amount the college pays a particular lecturer.

10: What is the college's income?

To help determine the amount of money earned by the college, details need to be recorded of the fees it charges students. As each course has its own set of charges, based on equipment etc., a field is required to record course prices. In addition, the amount paid by each student to attend the college needs to be recorded.

Course fee   Cost of a particular course

Enrolment fee   Amount paid by a student to enrol at the college. This will be a one off payment covering continuous attendance.

Course fees   Total amount payable by the student based on courses taken.

Total charged   The total amount paid by the student for education.

Now that the fields and some information concerning their formats have been determined it is possible to plan the design of the forms. During the above deliberations it became apparent that fields such as Home Address would appear on more than one form. This is not a problem as each form considers its fields to be unique and will not mistake them for a field with the same title on another form.

Earlier it was suggested that just three forms would be required: Student, Lecturer, and Course. However, in order to provide answers to all the questions raised above, the database will require another two forms – one to record the courses a particular student attends, the other to hold information regarding the courses conducted by a lecturer. These can be named Student Courses and Lecturer Courses respectively.

By now you are hopefully itching to start on your first form. So select option 1 Form Definition from the menu and let's get started!

DataEase will respond by asking you for the name of the form to be defined. As the first form we are going to design is the one that's going to hold course information then *Course* is the name that needs to be entered. Having checked that a form by that name is not already known to the database (it would complain if one did) DataEase continues by presenting us with an almost totally blank screen upon which we are going to build the new form.

Field Definition

Form design is one of the most enjoyable bits about constructing a DataEase database as you are free to play about as much as you wish, there being no screen layout rules to worry about. Fields can be placed anywhere on the screen you like, be it in columns, rows or higgledy-piggledy. DataEase is a very flexible database program and will not object. You are free to design the screen in whichever way you choose. However, a practice that can make life easier later on, is to think of the form as a display screen. Position the fields as you would wish to see them when accessing the database for information.

```
Form: COURSE              R  1 C   1
Form has 3 records, each 39 bytes, in file COURPAAA.DBM

COURSE TITLE                            COURSE NUMBER

OPTIMUM NUMBER OF STUDENTS      MAXIMUM NUMBER OF STUDENTS

ACTUAL NUMBER OF STUDENTS       MINIMUM NUMBER OF STUDENTS

COURSE REGISTRATION FEE




F4CMDHELP ESCEXIT F2SAVE F3CUT F5COPY F6PASTE F7DELLN F8INSLN F9SUBFRM F10FIELD
```

Layout of the Course form

Course Title

To position a field move the cursor, the white flashing blob, to where you wish the fields description to begin. It is usual to place some sort of description of a field's purpose next to it. In most cases the field's name is quite sufficient. You do not have to do this but it certainly makes field identification easier should amendments to the form be required later.

Having moved the cursor, using the arrow keys on the keyboard, to the required position, now type the field's name. The first field being defined on the Course form is named *Course Title*. Once that's been entered, press the spacebar twice to create a gap and then press <F10> on the right-hand side of the top row of the keyboard. This tells DataEase that you wish to describe a field.

You should now be seeing the Field Definition screen. Don't worry about your Form screen, it has not been lost, it's just having a break while this screen is displayed and will return intact later on. In effect the Field Definition screen is simply a form that's been designed by the people who wrote the DataEase program. Yes, DataEase itself uses its own database in order to help you design yours. Rather a tidy idea!

The first thing it wants to know is the name of the field. As DataEase expects the field's name to have been used as the description it treats that as the default value. It can be amended if you wish, but bear in mind the following rules:

❑ Names have a maximum size of 20 characters

❑ They can consist of letters, numbers and spaces

❑ Do not use punctuation marks (They have a special meaning to DataEase when used in procedures)

❑ Duplicate field names on the same form are not allowed

❑ DataEase cannot distinguish between upper and lower case letters so *COURSE TITLE* and *Course Title* would both be considered the same field name

❑ Do not use DataEase key names. These are any words used as part of the DQL language – see the Appendix for a complete list.

As we followed the expected practice it is only necessary to press <Enter> to move down to the next field.

Field Type

This is a choice field and can be one of any of eight types. Press <F1> for them to be displayed at the top of the screen.

Text

Any characters, including numbers but excluding the specific characters * ? and ~ which are treated as *wildcard* values by DataEase, can be considered to be text. The maximum length for a text field is 255 characters.Example use: Christian name

Numeric string

These are special fields designed to hold numbers that have a special format, such as a phone number, and that are not required to be used mathematically. If selected, an additional question will be asked seeking details concerning the field's special format. DataEase has three set formats plus one that you can set up for yourself:

No   This means that the data has no special format, for example the field Student Number will be an unformatted numeric string.

Soc.Set.No   A format that reveals DataEase's American origins. It sets up a field with the format 000-00-0000.

Phone No   Again unfortunately the phone format referred to here follows USA lines rather than UK. The field will be set up in this format (000)-000-000.

Other   A custom format that you can set yourself using zeros to show every digit position and the exact punctuation marks you require. For example, in order to set up a British style Phone No field the description could be (0000)-000000.

Number

This type is intended for fields whose use will involve calculations. It has three possible number types, each accurate up to 14 digits. Example: Optimum Class Size

Integer   Used for fields containing whole numbers and can be positive, negative or zero. If a field is to be signed (i.e. display of negative sign required) make sure that it is large enough to display all the required digits plus the sign.

Fixed Point   If the number of digits to the right and left of the decimal point can be pre-determined, use this number type for decimal fields. Be aware that DataEase adds a decimal point and a position for a comma to the left of the decimal point for every third digit so positioned. This means that the true length of a Fixed Point number will be longer than the number of digits specified. For example a field with seven digits to the left of the decimal and two to the right will take up 12 places on the screen. e.g 1,234,567.12.

Floating Point   A format that allows the number of digits upon either side of the decimal point to be variable. Although DataEase will not insert commas into floating point numbers always remember to allow a position for the decimal point when calculating the field's size.

Date

This format, not surprisingly, will hold a date. The default style is MM/DD/YY not as you might expect DD/MM/YY, again the American authors are the ones to blame. If this is a problem to you then the default value can be easily adjusted to DD/MM/YY by amending the System Configuration form. This is accessed via option 7 of the Main menu and Option 2 of the subsequent menu. The form extends over five screens, each accessed in turn by pressing <PgUp>. The system date field has a choice format and appears on the second page.

Time

Time fields appear in the format HH:MM:SS where HH = Hours, MM = Minutes and SS = seconds.

Pound

These fields could also be considered to be Fixed Point Number fields except that you are confined to two positions to the right of the decimal point and 12 to the left. You will be requested to state how many digits are required to the left.

Yes/No

Selecting this field type will confine the field's contents to being just a Yes or No. Accordingly the field's length will always be three characters.

Choice

A very useful field type. Basically it describes a field that is to have a limited range of possible answers, such answers being established at the point the field is described. Up to 99 possible answers can be defined, each having a length of anything up to 60 characters. Example: Age Range where only answers of 18+ 21+ 30+ 40+ and 55+ will be accepted by DataEase.

The field, Course Title, is to be a text field and this can be indicated to DataEase by simply selecting option 1 from the list of possible Field Types provided.

In some cases DataEase is able to work out for itself the maximum number of screen positions a field is likely to take up, for example when a Field Type of Choice is selected. But some of the other options available will leave it stumped and it will have to ask for more information. A Field Type of Text causes such a situation to arise and DataEase is forced to ask how long the field is to be. The answer we worked out earlier, namely 25 characters.

Having obtained replies to all its mandatory questions DataEase is now curious to know more about the field that's being defined. Such interest is indicated by the list of supplementary questions displayed in the lower half of the screen. The rewards for satisfying its inquisitiveness can be quite substantial so although we could cease defining this particular field at this point, by pressing <F2>, it would be better to spend a few moments considering their possibilities. Remember though that any information provided to DataEase from this point on can be viewed as voluntary. There is no requirement for the questions to be answered at all, so feel free to pick and choose which you respond to and when.

```
┌─────────────────────────────────────────────────────────────────────────┐
│ Form: STUDENT              (INSERT)                                        │
│                                                                           │
│ SURNAME            CHRISTIAN NAMES                    TITLE      AGE       │
│ HOME ADDRESS                         TELEPHONE NUMBER                      │
│                                      DATE ENROLED                          │
│                                      STUDENT NUMBER                        │
│ POST CODE                                                                 │
│ WORK ADDRESS                         TELEPHONE NUMBER                      │
│                                      CONTACTED                             │
│                                      EMPLOYMENT                            │
│ POST CODE                            ENROLLMENT FEE                        │
│                                      COURSE FEES                           │
│                                      TOTAL CHARGED                         │
│ F4CMDHELP ESCEXIT F2SAVE F3CUT F5COPY F6PASTE F7DELLN F8INSLN F9SUBFRM F10FIELD │
└─────────────────────────────────────────────────────────────────────────┘
```

The Student form definition screen

Required

DataEase wants to know if this field has to be completed every time the form is filled in. An answer of Yes will mean that an error message will be displayed if ever this field is left empty after information has been entered elsewhere. A reply of No, on the other hand, will allow it to be either left blank or filled with data, whichever is required at the time.

Indexed

If a field is described as being Indexed, DataEase will be able to sort and retrieve its information very quickly. However, this characteristic should be used frugally as the size of database files increases dramatically with each field so defined, slowing down other database activities. It is recommended that no more than eight fields on any particular form should be so classified.

Unique

A useful property for a field to have as it causes DataEase to prevent automatically any duplicate records from being keyed. Should this occur, it will produce a screen message stating *Record already exists* and enquire if the original data is to be updated from the new information.

Derivation Formula

DataEase is quite an intelligent program and, if asked to do so, will work out many fields contents for itself, requiring no information to be entered via the keyboard.

For example, it can be trusted to work out the current date, before placing that information into the field of your choice. But it won't attempt to do so unless it's received specific instructions beforehand in reply to this question. Such instructions are grouped under the term Derivation Formula.

The program can perform four types of field derivation each being identified by the keyword used. A keyword is simply a word or phrase that has a special meaning to DataEase. The three used within Derivation Formula are named Calculate, Lookup and Sequence From. The fourth derivation action called Default does not require the use of a keyword.

Calculate

DataEase can calculate the value to be contained in a field by means of a formula created by you. A formula can contain Field Titles, Constant values, Relationships and the usual mathematical operators such as + and −. For example:

```
No of Students + No of Lecturers
```

is a formula that works out the value to be placed into a field named Total People.

Note: Field names used inside a formula do not have to be on the form being designed. Using Relationships, field values can be taken off other forms.

Lookup

DataEase can Lookup the value of a field held upon another form and place that value into a field on this new form. However, a Relationship must exist between the two forms in question before a Lookup calculation will work.

Relationships are not covered until later in this chapter so for now just think of them as being chains that link forms.

DataEase is very flexible about when the Relationship is established as long as it has been defined before any attempt is made to use it. Otherwise its expresses its displeasure by displaying an error message that reads *Unknown Relationship* and the field will not be updated with any data. This flexible approach allows Lookup instructions to be issued before any Relationship has been recorded upon the database.

The Lookup instruction has certain rules governing its construction in the same way as grammar controls how a sentence should be written. The format to be followed consists of just three elements.

```
Lookup <Form Name> <Field Name>
```

Example:

```
LOOKUP STUDENT TITLE
```

This tells DataEase to find the first related Student form and then get the value held in the field named Title upon that form.

Just remember the order: first the command Lookup, then the name of the form that holds the field from which you want to get data, and then the name of the field that contains the required information upon that form.

The example above is the Lookup instruction in its simplest format. There is a further refinement to the command that requires the use of quote marks. Should the Form name consist of more than one word, its title must be contained within quote marks. The same rule applies to Field names.

Examples:

```
LOOKUP "STUDENT COURSES" COURSE
```

tells DataEase to get the form named Student Courses and copy data from the field named Course.

```
LOOKUP STUDENT "CHRISTIAN NAMES"
```

requests the form named Student to be obtained in order to access the information contained in a field named Christian Names.

```
LOOKUP "STUDENT COURSES" "COURSE NUMBER"
```

the extreme example where both Form and Field name consist of more than one word, instructs DataEase to find the Form named Student Courses and copy the data from the field named Course Number.

DataEase has some special keywords that can be used with the Lookup command. These are called Current Functions. There are five of them and they provide the following information:

Current Date
This will place the current date into the field. Note – the date recorded will be that understood by the computer to be the current date. This can be amended using the DOS command, Date, outside this program.

Current Time

Places the current time as known to the computer in the field being described. The DOS command, Time, will adjust the setting of the computer's clock.

Current User Name

The name of the person using DataEase is recorded as they enter the program. It is held inside a field named Current User Name. Via this function it is possible to record that person's identity upon any form that they insert or amend. Such information could be usefully used to provide an audit trail.

Current User Level

Another function that provides audit trail information. It records the security level of the person using DataEase upon the form.

Current Computername

This function is only available if DataEase is being used on a network. It records the identity of the computer being used to update the form.

Example:

```
LOOKUP CURRENT USER NAME
```

Note that there is no requirement to put quotes around Current Function keywords.

```
Form: LECTURER COURSE        R   1 C   1
Form has 5 records, each 62 bytes, in file LECTPAAB.DBM

  LECTURER NUMBER

            TITLE        CHRISTIAN NAMES              SURNAME

  COURSE NUMBER          COURSE TITLE












  F4CMDHELP ESCEXIT F2SAVE F3CUT F5COPY F6PASTE F7DELLN F8INSLN F9SUBFRM F10FIELD
```

The Lecturer Course form definition

Sequence

Sometimes all that we want a field to contain is a number or identity that increases in value as the field is used, an example being a membership number. DataEase will happily do this for you. All it requires to know is what number or code to start from.

This we can tell it using the Sequence command. Like the Lookup instruction this consists of three parts: the words Sequence From and then the start value which can be either a text or numeric value.

Example:

```
SEQUENCE FROM 1
```

Means that DataEase will give the field a value of 1 when it is first used, a value of 2 the second time it is used and then 3 and so on.

```
SEQUENCE FROM A1
```

This will run the sequence A1 to A9, then B1 to B9 then C1 to C9 and so on.

```
SEQUENCE FROM 1A
```

Starts the sequence at 1A changing to 1B then 1C all the way through to 1Z then it changes to 2A,2B etc.

Default

A constant value can be assigned to a field as its default value – a setting that can be overwritten by the user if required. It may be a number or text and is set by simply typing the value required. No keyword such as Lookup is needed.

Prevent Data-Entry

It is usual for this characteristic to be associated with fields that also have Derivation Formulae as it prevents users from overwriting the value of a field. After all, if you have gone to the trouble of telling DataEase how to calculate a field's contents, you would not then be likely to want anyone to come along and change that data, especially where such fields contain audit information.

A field can be set to prevent data-entry simply by replying *Yes* or *Yes, and do not save (virtual)* to this question.

There is a subtle difference between these two answers. A response of Yes will cause DataEase to only calculate the value of the field in question once. This happens the first time any information is recorded upon the form.

However, if you were to reply *Yes, and do not save (virtual)* DataEase will cheerfully recalculate the value of that field every time its form is looked at or used in a procedure. Therefore as the value contained within this field cannot be permanent DataEase will see no point in wasting disk space recording its value. So this response will both save disk space and allow the data to be flexible.

Example:

A field is required to hold the total amount paid by a student to be educated by the college. Being a total of two amounts, the college registration fee and the course charges, it's named Total Charged and it will have a derivation formula of:

```
ENROLMENT FEE + COURSE FEES
```

Obviously it is important that this field's value is not overwritten, therefore it needs to BE protected by being described as a field that prevents data-entry.

Response	Result
No	Data can be overwritten
Yes	Data cannot be overwritten The Total Charged value will remain as it was first calculated and never change.
Yes,and do not save (virtual)	The Total Charged value will be recalculated every time the form is used. Therefore should ever the college registration fee or course charge figures be amended this field will be automatically updated to reflect the new total figure.

Upper/Lower Limit

By the use of these field characteristics it is possible to control the range of values that can be entered into a field. Both values can be set or just one as the situation requires. DataEase automatically checks for silly errors such as setting a lower limit figure above that of the upper figure.

Limits can be detailed in many ways, the most common, of course, being numbers or text. But DataEase will also allow formulae or even the Lookup command to be used so a limit can be based upon a field held upon another form.

View/Write Security

We are now discussing DataEase's more exotic field characteristics. These two are concerned with data security.

Among the criteria to be considered when setting up a database is the question of how it is to be used in physical terms – deciding what controls you wish to apply to its use. For example, do you want everyone to be able to insert and delete data or is some of the information sensitive and, therefore, only to be seen by certain people?

DataEase provides a number of means by which these controls can be set up. Most are detailed in later chapters, but these two can be discussed now. Basically they are used to hide a specific field's contents from view while allowing the rest of a form's fields to be displayed.

This can be extremely useful. Take as an example the Salary field that we are going to use to hold information concerning how much the college pays each lecturer. Pay is generally a pretty sensitive issue and problems are likely to arise if this type of data were to be freely available to all users of the database.

It's been decided that the salary figures are to be recorded upon the same form as a lecturer's address details. Two people will have access to this form: a secretary and the Dean of the college. We want the Dean, but not the secretary, to be able to see the salary data. The View Security field characteristic will help us perform this magical slight of hand.

First, though, it's necessary for you to understand the principle of User levels. There are seven such levels, each providing data security, that range from High to Low 3. These govern how much a person can do within the database. You, as the owner of the database, are automatically given the highest rating. Thus you have complete control of the database and are allowed to decide which ratings should be applied to other people as you choose to introduce them to the database.

The default setting for View security is Low 3, while that for Write security is Medium 3. DataEase will allow everyone upon the specified security level, and above, to see/amend the value of the field. To anyone else it will just be a blank area of the form.

Thus to hide the salary information from the secretary, first that secretary would need to be allocated a security class lower than that of the Dean. Then the Salary field's View Security setting would have to be set to the same rating as the Dean.

A field's security access level is established by selecting a security setting from the list provided.

View Security is used to hide a field's contents.

Write Security is used to prevent a field's content from being altered by unauthorised personnel.

Field Help

Although hopefully by the end of this book you will be a DataEase expert that won't be true for the majority of people who are going to make use of your database.

Accordingly there are going to be more than a few occasions when cries for help will be hurled in your direction. Once more DataEase comes to the rescue!

It allows you to write a unique help message for each field on the form. The person using the database accesses this information by pressing the keys <Alt> and <F1> at the same time. The message you provide can be quite extensive as DataEase supports up to 19 lines (each 70 characters wide) of text. That's some 1,330 characters.

Now looking at the Field Definition screen it's quite evident that such a long message cannot be accommodated within the short area provided. Don't worry, press <F1> and DataEase will open a special screen, a window, within which you can type the message to be displayed.

Generally any help message will be displayed near the bottom of the screen. However, it can be positioned elsewhere if required, perhaps to prevent it obscuring the field in question. This is achieved by providing positioning information to DataEase at the start of the message. The program recognises this as an instruction to create a special window to contain your message.

The window information consists of numbers W, R, C, L where:

W = The number of characters in the longest line

R = The row in which you wish the top line of the message to appear

C = The column within which you want the message to start

L = The number of lines

Example:

The message *Enter the Student's Surname* is required to be displayed on the second line of the screen, four characters across from the first column:

❏ The text is 26 characters long: W = 26

❏ Row 1 is at the top of the screen so the second line will be row 2: R = 2

❏ It is to be displayed five characters in, 1 character = 1 column: C = 5

❏ The message is contained within one line: L = 1

Therefore, the message needs to be typed in as:

```
26,2,5,1 Enter the Student's Surname
```

Note: In order for DataEase to provide the Help function keys associated with Help text the minimum text length is 35. Where, as in the example above, the value of W is less than 35, DataEase will overwrite that figure with a value of 35.

Field Color

This field property, despite its American spelling, allows the colour attributes of the field to be changed. A field has two such attributes: Foreground controls the colour of the text, while the other, called Background, manages the colour of its background. By default, a field is displayed with yellow text (foreground) on a blue background. These can be changed by amending the field's colour description as shown in Table 2.1.

Table 2.1: Field colour descriptions

Description	Text	Background
Regular	Yellow	Blue
Highlight 1	White	Red
Highlight 2	Yellow	Black
Highlight 3	Black	Black
Title area	Yellow	Black
Mode area	Cyan	Black
Message area	Red	Black
Prompt line	Black	Green
Menu highlight	White	Blue
Key names	White	Red
Normal	Yellow	Black

Hide from Table View

One of the ways it is possible to view forms is to have their field contents displayed in a tabular format. This makes it very easy to see a number of forms at the same time. The Hide from Table View facility is similar to the View Security property in that it can be used to hide a field's contents when its form is being viewed inside a table.

Course Number

Now that we've seen all the properties that it is possible to assign a field, it's time to save the one we've just defined. This is achieved by simply pressing <F2>. DataEase will now return us to the Form definition screen where our Course Title field is looking rather lonely. So let's press on to define the next field.

Staying on the same line but pressing the spacebar a few times to create a gap, type its description, namely Course Number. This establishes the practice that will be followed throughout the construction of the Porterhouse database of providing field descriptions that match the field's name.

This field is to contain the unique course reference number. As such it will be a sequence field that is to start from the number 1. Having typed the name of the field now press <F10> to define that field's properties.

Once again the Field Definition screen is displayed for completion. The name of the field is to stand so press <Enter> or <Tab> to move down to the Field Type property. In order for the Course Number field to be a sequence field its format needs to be described as a Numeric String rather than a Number. So select that description from the options offered by pressing the number 2.

DataEase will now require to know if the field has a special format, listing four suggested answers. As it has no special format, opt for the first answer from those offered by pressing the number 1 on the keyboard.

You will next be asked to state how long the field is to be. Porterhouse, not being a major college, offers around 50 different courses to its students. So an answer of 2 characters would suffice. However, the Dean is ambitious, so a response of 3 will allow for any future expansion. Although making allowances such as this when calculating field sizes can mean waste of data space, it does help keep future database changes down to a minimum.

As the field's data is to be calculated by DataEase for us there's no need to make it a required field. Indexing is also not needed as the forms will be stored in sequence anyway. Unique? . . . for safety's sake we had better answer Yes to that question. Although in theory no sequence number should ever be repeated, were some Course forms to be deleted, this number's integrity could be put at risk.

Derivation formula? . . . a most definite Yes. This is where we explain to DataEase how to calculate the number that is to be stored in this field. Think about the number we want . . . it is to increase in value as each Course form is completed and the first such form is to be numbered 1. Therefore the derivation formula required reads:

```
SEQUENCE FROM 1
```

Finally, as we do not want that value to be overwritten, set the Prevent Data Entry property to Yes as well. None of the other field properties being required, press <F2> to save the field description and return to the Form Definition screen.

View or Modify a Form

Although there are still another five fields to be defined upon this form, let's take this opportunity to save the work so far completed by pressing <F2> again. This will result in our being returned to the Form Definition and Relationships menu.

The reason I've returned to the menu at this point is to discuss its second menu option *View or Modify a Form*. This option allows any form that has already been partly or fully designed to have fields added, amended or deleted. So it is possible for us to continue to add the remaining fields to the Course form while covering the processing available within this option.

So select option 2 from this menu by pressing that number on the keyboard. DataEase will respond by splitting the screen into three areas. The largest to the left and top of the screen still displays the Form Definition menu. At the bottom of the screen is a prompt area where DataEase is enquiring which form you wish to access. Positioned on the right is a column listing all the Forms so far designed.

There are two methods by which you can inform DataEase of your choice of form. The easiest is simply to type its number but if you prefer, the highlight bar can be moved up and down the column using the cursor keys until the name of the form you require is covered. Should you have constructed a database with a large number of forms, too many for DataEase to display all at one time, pressing <PgDn> will result in the additional form titles displayed. <PgUp>, of course, returns to the previous title column. The <Home> and <End> keys also play a part, providing a quick method of moving to and from the top and bottom of the column.

Once you've highlighted the form you require, in this case Course, press <Enter> for that form to be displayed. If, for some reason, you ever make a mistake at this point and select the wrong form, just press <F2> and you will be safely returned to the Form Definition menu with no damage done.

The five fields still to be placed on this form are the four concerning student numbers: Optimum, Maximum, Actual and Minimum Number of Students plus the field to contain the Course Registration Fee. So position the cursor, using the cursor keys, until it is covering the C of Course Title, then move it straight down two lines.

The field's description/name of Optimum Number of Students now needs to be typed before the cursor is moved two spaces forward using the spacebar. Press <F10> and once more we are back with the Field Definition screen which is probably beginning to look a bit familiar to you.

The field's name we are already happy with so press <Tab> to move down to the Field Type property. Now this is to be our first Number type field, so select the third field type description by pressing the number 3. You will now be asked whether the field is an Integer, Fixed Point or Floating Point. As the optimum number is a whole number the answer required is Integer, so press number 1 to select that description.

DataEase, as you might be beginning to appreciate, is quite a user-friendly program. Whenever it wishes to know something it usually provides you with a list of acceptable answers to choose from. You indicate your choice by pressing the numbers associated with the answers you wish to make. The program continues to provide this type of decision-making process throughout every level of its processing. This makes life a lot easier for us humans!

```
Form: LECTURER                 R  1 C   1
Form has 0 records, each 159 bytes, in file LECTPAAA.DBM

SURNAME              CHRISTIAN NAMES                   TITLE        AGE

HOME ADDRESS                        TELEPHONE NUMBER

                                    DATE EMPLOYED

                                    STAFF NUMBER

POST CODE                           PREVIOUS POST

SALARY




F4CMDHELP ESCEXIT F2SAVE F3CUT F5COPY F6PASTE F7DELLN F8INSLN F9SUBFRM F10FIELD
```

Design of the Lecturer form

Having told DataEase that it is dealing with an Integer it now wants to know the *Maximum number of digits in the field.* Porterhouse College does not go in for big classes so two digits will be quite sufficient, therefore respond by pressing the number 2 and then <Enter>. As this field is bog standard there is no need to provide any more detail, so press <F2> to return to the Form Definition screen ready to describe the next field, Maximum Number of Students.

This field and the remaining two student number fields have exactly the same description and properties as the Optimum Number of Students field we've just described. So now it's time for you to go solo for the first time and describe them to

DataEase by yourself. Just follow the procedures described in the previous four paragraphs and you'll be fine.

Once that's been done there's just the Course Registration Fee field to worry about. I trust that you are feeling confident after stretching your wings just now because you are going to be asked to do it again. I'm just going to describe this field's properties and then leave you to play with the skills you are developing.

Course Registration Fee

Field Type	**Number**
	Fixed point
	Digits to left of decimal = 3
	Digits to right of Decimal = 2

Congratulations, you've just constructed your first DataEase form. I hope it didn't cause too many problems but if you are still a little uncertain don't worry. There are plenty more opportunities to practice later on.

For now press <F2> to save the form's description upon the database and return to the Form Definition Menu. As you've seen option 2 of this menu, *View or Modify a Form*, is very similar to its predecessor *Define a Form*. Both provide the facility to describe Forms and the Fields they contain. Obviously it is not possible to Amend a form until its been defined, but, that apart, both options can be used in the construction of a form.

Incidentally, if you do go back to amend a form's design, when you come to re-save it DataEase will ask if you want to save the modified form under another name. This can be a useful cheat when constructing a number of forms that differ from each other only in minor ways. Build one, save it, amend it before saving it again under another name, and you now have two forms defined on the database!

If you do respond with a Yes, you will be prompted to supply the new form name. Should any information have already been placed upon the original form DataEase will provide you with the opportunity to copy that data on to the new form.

Hot Keys

While defining your form you may have noticed at the bottom of the Form Definition screen a selection of command prompts. These are DataEase's Hot Keys. They initiate some very useful processing at the touch of a single key.

F4 – Command Help

Pressing <F4> will result in the Command Menu overwriting part of the screen. To make a selection from that menu either move the highlight bar down to cover your choice and press <Enter> or press the keys detailed. This menu will then disappear.

Alt & F1 – Function Help

DataEase itself makes use of a database and therefore just as we are able to associate Help text with fields and forms, so were its designers. This means that a lot of helpful information can be provided by DataEase itself in response to the keys <Alt> and <F1> being pressed together. Usually the information it provides will be relevant to the function you are trying to perform at the time. This can be very useful.

Note: Some other pop-down menus can be accessed by pressing the left and right cursor keys. The functions provided by these menus will be covered later in the book.

F2 – Save and Exit

This key will cause the current field or form (dependent upon which is being described at the time) to be stored by DataEase. It can then be accessed again whenever it is needed. If no text or fields have been created then DataEase will record a blank form.

Esc – Exit and Abandon

Warning: Be very careful how you treat this button as it will return you to the previous screen or menu without saving any of your work. If you have just spent 10 minutes describing a field and then press <Esc> all that effort will have been wasted. However, there is a fail-safe mechanism as DataEase, always cautious, asks you to confirm this action before it proceeds to follow your instruction.

This facility to abandon what you are doing can be very handy especially if after making a few modifications to a form you decide that you really liked it better the way it was before.

F3 – Cut

Occasionally after you have finished a form you might examine it and decide that it would look better if a field was in another position, or perhaps that you could do without it all together. This Hot Key can be used to either move fields around a screen or to delete them.

First the Move:

1. Position the cursor at the start of the screen area you wish to move, usually at the start of the field's description.

2. Press <F3>.

3. Now move the cursor to the end of the area to be moved, say the end of the blue block that reveals how much room the field takes up on the screen.

4. Press <F3> again. The area in between the two places you marked with F3 will now disappear. Also any other text or fields upon that same line will move across to fill the gap so created.

5. Move the cursor to the place on the screen where you wish the field to re-appear, making sure there is enough room to accommodate it.

6. Press <F6> and the field will spring back into view.

7. Tidy up the screen if necessary. The <Insert> key will allow you to move fields to the right across the screen and the <Delete> key will move them to the left.

☛   **Tip:** Use the <F3> facility to move fields up and down the screen, but utilise the <Insert> and <Delete> keys instead to shuffle fields along a line.

Now the Delete:

1. Follow steps 1 to 4 as in the Move sequence.

2. Press <Esc> and the screen area contained within the <F3> markers will be removed from the form.

Note: Should <Esc> be pressed before step 4 the Hot Key action will be aborted.

F5 – Copy

A very useful key this and very powerful. It copies text, fields and forms. Its ability to handle forms will be explored and put to good use in the next chapter when data entry is discussed. Here are the steps to be followed in order to copy a piece of text or a field:

1. Position the cursor at the beginning of the area you wish to copy.

2. Press <F5>.

3. DataEase will ask if you want to copy a Block, a Form, a Dictionary Field, or None.

None: Abandons the Copy action.

Form: Copies a Form that's already been described, into the screen.

Block: Copies a screen area.

Dictionary: Allows a field that's been described upon the Dictionary to be copied onto the screen. The Dictionary is a form supplied by DataEase upon which fields common to many other forms can be defined. Then having been so described they can then be copied as many times as may be required onto other forms. This form can be accessed in the exactly the same way as its fellow forms.

4. Select Block.

5. Now move the cursor to the end of the area to be copied.

6. Press <F5> again.

7. Move the cursor to where the copy is to be made.

8. Press <F6> and the copied code will appear on the screen.

9. Having already marked the block with F5 there is no need to do so again if the same area is to be copied immediately to somewhere else. Simply repeat steps 7 and 8 as many times as required

F7 – Delete

Use this key to Delete the entire line upon which the cursor rests. Note there is no need to move the cursor to the start or end positions before pressing <F7>. Be very careful when using this key as there is no way to restore a line that's been deleted. Apart that is, from pressing <Esc> which, while it will restore the form to its original state, will also mean the loss of any other changes you've made.

F8 – Insert

Pressing <F8> will result in a blank line being inserted onto the screen pushing the line upon which the cursor currently rests down a line.

F9 – Subform

It is possible for forms to appear within forms, such forms being referred to as Subforms. This key is used to mark where they are to be positioned upon the parent form.

F10 – Define a Field

Provides access to the Field Definition screen where a field's properties can be accessed.

Porterhouse Forms

There are five Forms in all within the Porterhouse database that need to be described. Listed below are details of each and the fields they are to contain. Please use this information to build these forms by yourself. They will be needed later on in the book when it comes to describe how to access and process data held on the database. In addition once you've successfully built these forms you can be confident that you have the skills and the knowledge to construct your own forms when that time arrives. Besides, it provides a chance for you to play with some of the Hot Keys described above. The Dictionary might also be put to good use !

All the field formats that you will encounter have been covered but a bit more detail concerning Choice fields is required before you get started. The Title field has such a format and as it appears upon a number of forms it seems an obvious one to be used a an example. We'll pick up the story as the Field Definition form appears on the screen.

The Field Name will be Title and as that's already the default value it can be safely left to stand, allowing us to move down on to the Field Type property. Now if you look across the top of the screen you should see a number of field type descriptions listed. You'll notice that Choice is not among them. Don't worry, it is available – there's just insufficient room upon the screen to display all the field type titles this way. This is indicated by DataEase inviting you to press <F1> in order to view more options.

This should be done and as a result the descriptions will vanish from the top of the screen, being displayed instead inside a column that's just popped up into view on the screen's right. Now it can be seen that a Choice type description is provided as option 8. So key that number to continue. It is useful to note that once you know the number of an option that number can be keyed directly without you first having to display that option upon the screen.

DataEase will now be asking you to provide the *Optional choice type name*. In addition there is a prompt at the top of the screen stating *Press F1 to see list of choices*. This provides the simplest way of providing your choice options so press <F1>. The middle of the screen will now be taken up by a table, within which are listed a number of choice options all of which are blank. The cursor is happily blinking against the first such option waiting for some information to be keyed.

The Title field is to have seven possible answers namely: Mr, Mrs, Ms, Miss, Dr, Sir and Lady. These now have to be entered onto the table such that each title has its own unique option number – i.e. type a title then press <Enter> to allow the next title to be entered against the option below.

Once all the seven titles are in the table, press <F2> to return to the Field Definition form. Then press <F2> again to store that field's description upon the form.

Now, here as promised, is the list of the remaining forms and their fields.

Note: Where *Other Format* appears in the Size column the description of that format will be detailed alongside it.

Example:

Other Format (0000) means that (0000) should be keyed as the format for that field.

Form = Student

Field	Format	Size
Surname	Text	12 characters
Christian names	Text	14 characters
Title	Choice	Mr Mrs Ms Miss Dr Sir Lady
Age range	Choice	18+ 21+ 30+ 40+ 55+
Home address line 1	Text	20 characters
Home address line 2	Text	20 characters
Home address line 3	Text	20 characters
Home address line 4	Text	20 characters
Home postcode	Text	8 characters
Home tel code	Numeric String	Other format (0000)
Home tel no	Numeric String	Other format 000000
Date enrolled	Date	Defaults
Student number	Numeric String	4 digits Formatted string = No Derivation Formula Sequence from 1
Work address line 1	Text	20 characters
Work address line 2	Text	20 characters
Work address line 3	Text	20 characters

Work address line 4	Text	20 characters
Work postcode	Text	8 characters
Work tel code	Numeric String	Other format (0000)
Work tel no	Numeric String	Other format 000000
Work Ext	Numeric String	Other format 0000
Contacted	Choice	Word of Mouth
		Local Paper
		Mailshot
		Radio Advert
		Other
Employment	Choice	Self Employed
		Business
		Student
		Unemployed
		Other
Enrolment fee	Number	Fixed point
		Digits to left of decimal = 2
		Digits to the right = 2
Course fees	Number	Fixed point
		Digits to left of decimal = 4
		Digits to the right = 2
Total charged	Number	Fixed point
		Digits to left of decimal = 4
		Digits to the right = 2

Form = Lecturer

Field	Format	Size
Surname	Text	12 characters

Christian names	Text	14 characters
Title	Choice	Mr Mrs Ms Miss Dr Sir Lady
Age	Number	Integer 2 digits
Home address line 1	Text	20 characters
Home address line 2	Text	20 characters
Home address line 3	Text	20 characters
Home address line 4	Text	20 characters
Home postcode	Text	8 characters
Home tel code	Numeric	Other format (0000)
	String	
Home tel no	Numeric	Other format 000000
	String	
Lecturer number	Numeric	4 digits
	String	Formatted String = No
		Derivation Formula
		Sequence from *1*
Previous post	Text	15 characters
Salary	Number	Integer 6 digits
Date employed	Date	

Form = Student Courses

Field	Format	Size
Student number	Numeric	4 digits
	String	Formatted String = No
Title	Choice	Mr Mrs Ms Miss Dr Sir Lady
Christian names	Text	14 characters
Surname	Text	12 characters
Course number	Numeric	3 digits
	String	Formatted String = No
Course title	Text	25 characters

Form – Lecturer Course

Field	Format	Size
Lecturer number	Numeric	4 digits
	String	Formatted String = No
		Derivation Formula
Title	Choice	Mr Mrs Ms Miss Dr Sir Lady
Christian names	Text	14 characters
Surname	Text	12 characters
Course number	Numeric	3 digits
	String	Formatted String = No
Course title	Text	25 characters

Relationships

What are relationships and how do they work? In Chapter 1 mention was made of records being linked to form chains. Relationships can be thought of as the links in those chains. They connect one form to another so that information contained upon one form can be accessed and used by the other. This facility helps save both time and precious data space: Time, because information can be provided to the database on a single form, rather than being spread around a number of forms, and space because as the information is only recorded on the one form it need only be stored in one place by the computer.

```
Relationships                        To skip the menu, press ESC.
1: System 2: LECTURER 3: LECTURER COURSE 4: COURSE 5: STUDENT         F1MORE
                          FORM RELATIONSHIP
BETWEEN
Form 1: STUDENT
If Form 1 is  Subform, how should Key
field  be  updated when Main form Key
is modified:
                                 & Form 2: STUDENT COURSES
                                   If Form 2 is  Subform, how should Key
                                   field  be  updated when Main form Key
                                   is modified:
BASED ON THE FOLLOWING FIELDS BEING EQUAL:  (Define at least one set)

      Field    STUDENT NUMBER        =       STUDENT NUMBER
   And Field                         =
   And Field                         =

OPTIONAL RELATIONSHIP NAMES:
        (Form names are used as a default.)

   for Form 1:STUDENT NUMBER MATCH   Form 2:STUDENT NUMBER MATCH

F4CMDHELP ESCEXIT F2SAVE Sh-F1TABLE F3VIEW F7DEL F8MODIFY F9QBE F10MULTI
```

The Relationship Definition screen

DataEase provides the facility to use Relationships and through them we can link any number of forms to pool their information. For example, using the services of the Lookup command, we can tell DataEase to find the Student Course record that satisfies the relationship criteria described in the relationship named Student Number Match (that we've still to describe) and then make available the information held in its Course Title field, possibly by copying it onto a screen field named Course Title.

Note: The two fields have the same name. This is not mandatory as DataEase will happily accept relationships between fields with differing names. But it does make your database more understandable if linked fields share a common title.

It is important however that both field descriptions match – i.e. they have the same Field Type and Field Length properties. Failure to adhere to this rule will result in the relationship not being recognised by DataEase and the error message *Unknown Relationship* will be displayed whenever an attempt to use the relationship is made.

DataEase understands two types of relationships, namely Ad-Hoc and Predefined. Ad-Hoc relationships have a temporary nature and will be covered more fully by a later chapter, while Predefined relationships have a permanent existence within the database, until either the database or they themselves are deleted.

We define such a relationship through the services offered by option 3 of the Form Definition menu, *Define Relationships.*

Form Relationship

The Define Relationships option takes us into a screen named Form Relationship. It is upon this screen that we describe the links we wish to build between our database forms. As just mentioned, a relationship named Student Number Match needs to be created so let's take a look at how to go about that task.

Relationship	Purpose
Student Number Match	Link Student form to Student Courses form
	Key field = Student number

Key fields were referred to in Chapter 1 as being the *hooks* by which records are attached to one another. This description now requires some expansion. Databases need some information to work on when they are asked to find a particular form. For example, there could be 1,000 students attending Porterhouse College, each with a Student form on the database. If asked to display a certain student's address how is DataEase to know which Student form we are interested in?

The answer is by using a field that uniquely identifies the student about whom we require information, in other words a key field. In this example, it would be possible to ask DataEase to search its files using the Surname field upon the Student form as the key field. However, surnames are not renowned for being unique, so we would likely have more than one student's address reported back to us by DataEase. Of course, we could narrow that search down by including the Christian Names field as well. DataEase can handle up to three identified key fields at the same time and any field on a form can be nominated as a key field. But duplication could still occur.

It is the Student Number field upon that form that should be used in this instance as the key field, because as it is incremented by one each time a student is registered by the college, its value will always be unique to each student.

Once provided with a student's ID number we can be confident that DataEase will conduct its search and return only the required Student form.

This is one use of key fields. Relationships use them slightly differently. Here they are used as indicators that identify the fields on the forms being linked that are to hold the same informational content – a relationship only existing between two forms if the key fields specified for that relationship contain values that match exactly. In other words, for the Student Number Match relationship to work the Student Number Field on both the Student form and the Student Courses form would have to contain the same number.

As stated above, key fields do not have to have the same name but they must have identical Field Type and Field Length properties for the matching process to work properly.

A relationship between two forms is established by responding to the questions posed by DataEase on this screen. So let's continue by defining the Student Number Match relationship.

Form 1

DataEase requires to know the name of the *parent* form in the relationship. In many cases it will not matter which form you use, but occasionally when the *child* form is a Subform the answer takes on more importance.

Along the top of the screen you will notice that DataEase has helpfully displayed the names of all the forms we've created. Press <F1> to have them displayed in a column and then select the Student form. Its name will then appear upon the screen in the box near to the question it answers.

If you wanted to describe a relationship for a form that has yet to be created, as DataEase will not have been able to display a name, you would need to press <Esc> instead at this point. The future form's name would then have to be entered into the box provided. This is a procedure that should also be followed if you are defining a relationship between a form and a Data Entry form (described later in the book).

If Form 1 is a Subform, how should the key field be updated when the Main form key is modified?

There are three possible responses to this question which is asking how you wish DataEase to handle Subform key field values if the parent form's key field values are updated.

Null   The usual answer for all occasions where there are no Subforms. It sets the Subform's key fields to blank should the parent key values change.

Cascade   This will cause the key field values on the Subform to be updated to match those on the parent. In addition should ever the parent form be deleted, so will all its related Subforms.

Restrict   This restricts the key field values update to just the parent form leaving those on the Subform unchanged.

Note: Null and Restrict effectively mean that the link between a parent and its related Subforms will be broken should the parent's key field values ever change.

As the Porterhouse database does not include any Subforms it is safe to leave this question unanswered and <Tab> onto the next question.

Form 2

Now DataEase wishes to know the name of the form to be linked to that named as Form 1. Again it has helpfully provided the form names at the top of the screen so select form Student Courses.

If Form 2 is a Subform, how should the key field be updated when the Main form key is modified?

The same criteria apply as when this question was asked of Form 1. Once more our response is to ignore the question and move onto DataEase's next query.

Based on the following fields being equal:

Here is where we tell DataEase which fields on our two forms are to be treated as key fields – i.e which field values to match when trying to find the linked records. Space is provided for three field *pairings* to be established, the maximum that DataEase can handle. And, once again DataEase is offering plenty of assistance by listing some field names at the top of the screen. Press <F1> to have them placed inside a column. You will notice that it has only listed those contained upon Form 1. This helps avoid a lot of confusion especially if, as recommended, you use the same field names across a number of forms.

In the case of the Student Number Match relationship only one key field pairing is required, using the Student Number field that appears upon both forms. Bearing that in mind, select that field from the list and see it displayed as Field 1 underneath Form 1.

Automatically DataEase will have moved across to the next column, that under Form 2, where it awaits a field to be selected from that form. It will also have changed the field names displayed at the head of the screen to those contained upon that form. Again select field Student Courses.

As no other fields on either form are to be linked continue pressing <Tab> until you reach the question at the base of the screen. If other fields were needed to establish a match it would just be necessary to repeat the above actions until either all three pairings had been established or your matching criteria had been satisfied.

Optional Relationship Names

If these fields on the screen are left blank DataEase will default the relationship name to that of the forms. However, if more than one relationship is to be established for a form, for example the Lecturer Course form has two relationships, one with the Course form and the other with the Lecturer form, a specific name must be given to each relationship.

Within the Porterhouse database the standard has been to apply a name to every relationship. In this case type Student Number Match.

The relationship has now been described and can be stored by pressing <F2>. A number of other relationships will be required during the construction of the Porterhouse database. In order to provide you with an opportunity to practice defining relationships here are a few for you to set up now.

The Forms marked with an asterisk (*) refer to a DQL procedure name rather than a database Form. This type of relationship will be explained in Chapter 5. For now, whenever an asterisked form name is to be entered, simply press <Esc> once, before going on to type the DQL procedure's name.

Relationship	Description
Costing	Form 1 = Student Courses
	Form 2 = Course
	Form 1 Field = Course Number
	Form 2 Field = Course Number
Course Number Match	Form 1 = Course
	* Form 2 = Xref Lecturer/Course

	Form 1 Field = Course Number
	Form 2 Field = Course Number
Course Link	Form 1 = Course
	* Form 2 = Xref Student/Courses
	Form 1 Field = Course Number
	Form 2 Field = Course Number
Student Link	Form 1 = Student
	* Form 2 = Xref Student/Courses
	Form 1 Field = Student Number
	Form 2 Field = Student Number
Course1	Form 1 = Course
	* Form 2 = Registration
	Form 1 Field = Course number
	Form 2 Field = Course number1
Course2	Form 1 = Course
	* Form 2 = Registration
	Form 1 Field = Course number
	Form 2 Field = Course number2
Course3	Form 1 = Course
	* Form 2 = Registration
	Form 1 Field = Course number
	Form 2 Field = Course number3
Course4	Form 1 = Course
	* Form 2 = Registration
	Form 1 Field = Course number
	Form 2 Field = Course number4
Course5	Form 1 = Course
	* Form 2 = Registration
	Form 1 Field = Course number
	Form 2 Field = Course number5

Some More Hot Keys

While describing the above Relationships and perhaps during the definition of some of the forms you may have noticed that the Hot Keys described earlier in this chapter had different legends against them to the ones I described. This occurred because DataEase adapts its Hot Keys to suit whatever action is being performed at the time. Here is some more information about them.

Shift-F1 – Table

One of the methods of viewing information stored on the database that will be discussed further in a later chapter is that of a table. Here the forms and their fields contents are displayed in columns. To access this facility just press these two keys together. In addition to letting you see the data, DataEase will also allow you to amend, delete or insert more information.

F3 – View

If more than one Relationship or Form has been described upon the database then it is possible to view them by pressing this key. DataEase will continue to display information in response to this key until no more data is available, when it will restart the display commencing with the first form/relationship recorded.

F7 – Delete

If this key is pressed the current information being displayed will be deleted from the database. DataEase will check back with you first to confirm that this is what is really required.

F8 – Modify

The first time information about a form is stored by DataEase it treats that process as Data Creation. Any subsequent amendments to that data it will treat as modifications. Therefore in order to save amended data onto the database it is necessary to press <F8> rather than <F2> you've become used to. Don't worry, DataEase can recognise when these keys have been used in the wrong place and will query your instruction before taking any action.

Delete a Form

The fourth option on the Form Definition menu provides the facility to delete a form off the database. It's use is very straightforward.

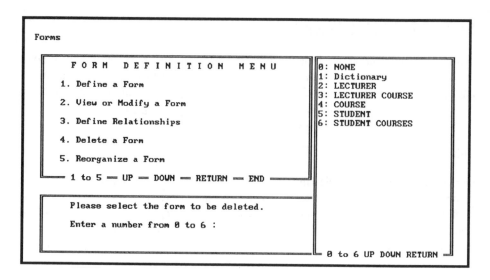

The Form Deletion screen

Simply select option 4 off the menu and DataEase will provide a list of all the forms it has described for the current database. Choose the form to be deleted from the titles supplied and then press <Enter>. DataEase will respond by displaying that form's name again at the bottom of the screen requesting that you confirm its deletion. The deletion can be cancelled by pressing either <N> or <Esc>. A reply of <Y> will result in the form and all its associated information being removed from the database.

Should a form be involved in any relationships, DataEase will also enquire if its associated forms and their data are to be deleted as well.

Reorganize a Form

The final option on this menu tidies up a form. By that I don't mean it makes them look any prettier, instead DataEase will read through its files removing any deleted information.

How can it find deleted data? Surely once informations been deleted it's gone from the database? Not quite, when DataEase is informed that a piece of information is no longer required, perhaps because it is in error or out of date, rather than get rid of it straight away it flags it as being marked for deletion. This means that should any data have been deleted in error DataEase can help you to restore it. Another example of how user friendly DataEase can be. It is aware that we humans have our off days and makes provision to save us from ourselves.

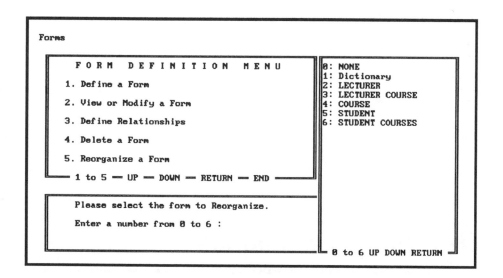

The Form Reorganisation screen

However it recognises that some information will have been genuinely deleted and so it has to provide a facility for this data to be removed from the database. This is what is meant by the term *Reorganize a Form*. DataEase scans through its files removing any information that's been marked for deletion. Incidentally, once a bit of data has been so flagged DataEase will totally ignore it during any subsequent searches or calculations, so to that degree it will have been deleted.

To implement the reorganisation of a form, first select this option from the menu and then choose the form to be treated from the list that DataEase provides. Once you've pressed <Enter> DataEase will do the rest, returning you to the Form Definition menu screen once it's completed its bit of housekeeping.

DataEase Capacities

To end this chapter here are a few facts concerning the form definition capacities of DataEase.

Forms per database	2,000
Records per form	16 million
Fields per form	255
Characters per field	255
Characters per record	4,000
Screens per form	16

3

Data Entry Techniques

Once the Forms have been designed and created within DataEase it is time to start thinking about how information is going to be recorded upon them. In other words what method of data entry we are going to employ. The term *data entry* is used to describe the process by which information is provided to a program or database.

There are two methods by which data can be entered onto your DataEase database. The first can be accessed via the Main menu and is used primarily by database supervisors (i.e. you), either to set up the initial information that is to be held by the database or during later maintenance operations. It is rarely made available to other users of the database.

The second facility, which is more sophisticated and to which access can be controlled by you to ensure that only authorised persons are able to insert information, is better suited for the purpose. It will be covered in depth later in this chapter after you have first had a bit of practice using the data entry techniques made available via option 2, *Record Entry*, of the DataEase Main menu.

Upon selecting this menu option you will be presented with a screen containing a list of all the forms that you described during Chapter 2. It will probably look fairly familiar as it has the same structure as the screen that controls the viewing or amendment of a form's layout. So you should not be surprised to find that it is used in the exactly the same way, except that this time you will be asked to identify the form that is to have some information recorded upon it. The selected form will then be displayed ready for data entry.

So, slipping back into our role as the Dean of Porterhouse College, let us start by setting up information pertaining to its staff, namely the Lecturers. Select the Lecturer form from those listed on the right-hand side of the screen.

DataEase will respond by displaying the Lecturer form and all its fields, ready for some information to be keyed. You'll also notice that at the base of the screen a number of Hot Keys are also detailed. More information on them will be provided later, for now let us just concentrate on getting some data recorded.

The cursor is flashing on the screen, within the field that we named Surname. This is the way that DataEase urges us to supply some information, in this case the surname of a Lecturer. So being totally original, type in the word *Brown* (don't worry, Smith will be used later as we come to record the college students!). Then signal to DataEase that that is all the data to be provided for that field by pressing either <Tab> or <Enter>. The cursor should now happily skip over to the next field where DataEase will await the entry of the lecturer's Christian names, *Colin James.*

```
LECTURER
New Record on Screen

SURNAME  BROWN           CHRISTIAN NAMES  COLIN JAMES      TITLE  DR     AGE  45

HOME ADDRESS  21 LOWER LANE          TELEPHONE NUMBER  (0271) 489924
              LITTLE NOLEDGE
              HANTS                  DATE EMPLOYED     01/09/87

                                     STAFF NUMBER      0001

POST CODE     LN0 H12                PREVIOUS POST     HARROW

SALARY        75,000




F4CMDHELP ESCEXIT F2SAVE Sh-F1TABLE F3VIEW F7DEL F8MODIFY F9QBE F10MULTI
```

Data entered upon the Lecturer form

Having supplied those names, press <Enter> again and the cursor will move along to the Title field. During the form design stage we informed DataEase that this field was to be a Choice field and we supplied a list of acceptable titles. DataEase now gently reminds us of this by helpfully listing all the titles we specified across the top of the screen, each with a reference number so it can be easily selected.

Should there ever be insufficient room across the screen for DataEase to display all the available options in a single line it will indicate that more choices are available by adding the <F1> key to the options displayed. If this key is pressed DataEase will create a column down the right-hand side of the screen, providing itself with more room in which to display the available options. Should there be more options than it can list in a single column, <PgDn> can be used to view more.

Note: DataEase will only accept an answer that's among those we have indicated as being acceptable. For example, it would object if you tried to supply a title of Duke as this was not included in our list of titles when we described the Choice field. If this title did need to be included it would be necessary to add it to the list by amending the form as described in Chapter 2.

You indicate your choice of Title to DataEase by keying its associated number. In this case our lecturer Mr Brown, being a Doctor of Philosophy, is used to being addressed as Dr and so that means we have to press the number 5 in order to have that title entered against this field.

The next data item to be keyed is the lecturer's age, so enter Dr Brown's as being 45. The cursor will now automatically move down the screen to the Home address fields.

The first address line is to read *21 Lower Lane* so enter that into the first field then press <Enter>. The cursor may now surprise you by not moving horizontally as might be expected down to the next address field, but instead opting to travel in a vertical direction across to the Telephone field. DataEase always works in this fashion, wanting all the fields on a line to be completed before it will move down to the next row of fields. Your form design, where possible, should bear this in mind. If it is an inconvenience now for you to keep breaking away from the address to supply other information, imagine how other less skilled users of your database will feel. Later on I will show you how to circumvent this problem when the other method of data entry is discussed.

The telephone number field has been split into two parts, the area code (contained within brackets) and the actual telephone number. Enter the code *0271* and then type Dr Brown's telephone number *489924*. You might have noticed that you didn't have to press <Enter> to move between these two fields. DataEase was simply being helpful and intelligent. As the first field had been completely filled, the four-digit area code being the maximum number of digits allowed, it automatically moved you across to the next field.

Incidentally, should you ever make a mistake while entering information it is possible to correct it by using a combination of the cursor, <Delete> and <Insert> keys. The cursor keys can be used to move you around the screen, jumping fields as required, the <Delete> key then being used to remove the highlighted character or instead the <Insert> key could be pressed in order to create a gap into which a character or digit is to be placed.

As the telephone field was also completely filled with digits, DataEase has automatically jumped down a line to the next field which is the second address line. The data to be keyed here is the name of the village where Dr Brown resides, namely *Little Noledge*, before moving on to the Date Employed field.

DataEase has already provided a clue as to the format of this field by breaking it up into three two-digit groups, each separated by a slash. DataEase supplies all dashes, decimal points, commas and so on when data is being entered, dependant, of course, upon the field's description. This makes life very simple when keying in a date as all that is required is to press the relevant numbers. In this case, as Dr Brown commenced work at the college on September 1st 1987, we need only key *010987* and DataEase will correctly record that as 01/09/87. For completeness, maybe the field could have included (dd/mm/yy) as part of its description on the screen. This would inform any user of the database that the date to be keyed needs to be in the format day/month/year.

Once that field has been completed you will find that DataEase has moved the cursor on two fields, completely by-passing the Staff Number field. Well that's not quite true because a value has appeared against that field of 0001. Now what caused that to happen?

It occurred because, as you may remember, that field was described with a Lookup property that told DataEase to automatically calculate a value for the field based on a sequence number that was to start from 1. So DataEase just followed instructions!

Next, the Postcode field should be completed with the code *LNO H12* and Dr Brown's previous post was at *Harrow*. That brings us onto the last field on the form that is titled Salary. Again all that is required is to type in the good Doctor's salary this being *75000*. Note that you only need to type in the digits, DataEase placing the comma in the correct position.

And that is really all there is to it. Data entry is really a very straightforward business, all the hard work having being done during the form design stage. To store the information we've just keyed, press <F2> and DataEase will update the database.

Here's the name and address details for another lecturer. Press <F5> to clear the screen and then have a go at recording this information on the database by yourself.

Dr Rosemary Bishop   Age 40   Telephone (0271) 665482

                                      156 Lincolns Way
                                      Gt Eyedills
                                      Hants
                                      GE4 H12

                                      Salary £50,000   Started 20th May 1988

                                      Previous Post: Barnstaple

Attention was drawn to the Hot Keys a little earlier and the time has now come for more detail to be revealed about a powerful facility that can be accessed via one such

key combination: the combined pressing of the <Shift> and <F1> keys. If these keys
are pressed a data entry table with a number of columns that spread right across the
screen will be displayed. Each column directly relates to each of the fields upon the
form in question.

You can see these field names displayed at the head of each column. Some will have
been abbreviated to the size of the field they describe, for example Title has been
reduced to four characters, Titl , that being the maximum entry size permissible for
that field. DataEase will attempt to fit in as many columns as it can across the screen,
but obviously sometimes it is going to run out of room before it has been able display
all the available fields.

This is not a problem, because as you access each field, DataEase will automatically
drop the left most column, replacing it with a new field area on the right-hand side of
the screen. Reverse your direction of travel across the screen and the replaced
columns will reappear.

```
LECTURER
New Record on Line 4 of 3

SURNAME      CHRISTIAN NAME  TITL  AG  HOME ADDRESS LINE 1   HOME T  HOME T  HOME ADD
BROWN        COLIN JAMES     DR    45  21 LOWER LANE         (0271)  489924  LITTLE N
BISHOP       ROSEMARY        DR    40  156 LINCOLNS WAY      (0271)  665482  GT EYEDI
STANTON      GEORGE          MR    35  45 RAYLEIGH ROAD      (0271)  447729  STANWAY
                                                             (    )
                                                             (    )
                                                             (    )
                                                             (    )
                                                             (    )
                                                             (    )
                                                             (    )
                                                             (    )
                                                             (    )
                                                             (    )
                                                             (    )
                                                             (    )
                                                             (    )
                                                             (    )

F4CMDHELP  ESCEXIT  F2SAVE  Sh-F1FORM  Ctrl-F5UNDO  F7DELETE  F10MULTI
```

The Data Entry Table screen

Press <Shift> and <F1> together now, and you will see the information we've so far
recorded on the database displayed upon the screen. However, the table does far more
than just display all the records associated with a particular form. It is also another
way of entering or amending data.

You can test this out now by pressing the <End> key. This tells DataEase to create
some extra lines for you on the table. Move the cursor until you are in the first clear

line within the column headed Surname and then start to enter information about our third lecturer, Mr George Stanton. Just as with the form display method detailed above, you type the information into each field and then press <Tab> or <Enter> to move across into the next column.

This provides a very quick way of keying information onto the database as once each line is completed you are automatically moved down to the next to start recording information about another lecturer. Each line in the table represents a Form Record. Do not press <F2> until you have recorded all the information that you want. DataEase will then write all the new data entered onto the table into the database in one go. It's a very efficient method of recording data.

Here is some more information about Mr Stanton that you can enter onto the database now to give yourself some practice in table data entry.

Mr George Stanton   Age 35   Telephone number 0271-447729

                                      45 Rayleigh Road
                                      Stanway
                                      Hants
                                      SW1 H05

                                      Salary £32,000   Started 16th August 1990

Incidentally, tables can also be used as a quick way to correct data. Just call up the table, then move the cursor to the field that requires amendment. Change its data, then press <Enter>. DataEase will indicate that it has accepted the amendment by highlighting the complete record. You can now move on to do more amendments or press <F2> to tell DataEase that it can update the database. Note that no amendments are applied to the actual database until <F2> has been pressed. This means that if you suddenly realise that you've corrected the wrong data, no permanent damage will have been done. Simply press <Esc> to cancel the update and then start again.

In Chapter 1, Records, Fields and Data were described. Records became known as Forms inside Chapter 2 and now you might have become confused by the term *Form Record* that has just been introduced. What is it?

A Form might only have data recorded upon it the once in which case there would be no need to concern ourselves with Form Records and the earlier simplistic approach, as practised within Chapter 2, of considering a Form to be a Record could continue unabated. However, as we have already seen demonstrated with the Lecturer form, it is far more probable that a form will have data recorded upon it a number of times.

Imagine a DataEase form to be a classroom blackboard. In the course of a lesson it becomes covered in chalk, in other words data has been entered onto it. Eventually it will require cleaning in order to make way for some more information. Immediately the blackboard duster begins to be used, the information contained upon that board would become lost, permanently . . . unless, that is, someone bothered to take a photograph of the board just before it was cleaned.

Enter DataEase as an electronic David Bailey. It captures each *blackboard* as a snapshot just before it clears the screen. These *snaps*, or Form Records, are then stored away inside a photo album (database) that's uniquely associated with the Form in question.

User Friendly Data Entry

Now, the methods described above are the easiest and most straightforward way of recording information upon your database. But, as was said earlier, there are data security implications concerning their use and data has to be entered in the order that fields are displayed.

You are now about to encounter DataEase's own programming language DQL for the first time. If the thought of doing a bit of computer programming has you reaching for a Stephen King novel for a bit of light relief, PUT IT DOWN!! There's nothing to be afraid of, and you might even come to enjoy it!

When computers were going through their dinosaur stage of evolution you might well have had reason for an arm's length attitude towards them. Then you had to be a devoted acolyte with a million degrees in mathematics before they would even tell you the time of day. They had huge valves and bulbs and worked very slowly. Incidentally the term *bug* used by programmers to describe a fault in a program came into use after a large flying insect became attracted to a glowing valve in an American computer. Its romantic intentions came to an abrupt, if interesting end, when the machine responded with a pyrotechnic display that climaxed with a blown fuse!

But times change, and computers and their software with them. How the term *user friendly* first sprang into being I don't know, but the authors of DataEase certainly had it at the front of their minds when they wrote the software, and this is reflected in the DQL (DataEase Query Language) that they have supplied.

We'll start by returning to the DataEase Main menu and selecting option 4, *DQL Advanced Programming*. True to form, DataEase promptly responds with yet another menu screen, the DQL Menu. This details 10 different menu selections, plus of course <Esc> that would return us to the Main Menu.

Ignoring option 1, *Run Procedure*, (we have no choice as we've not written one yet!), select the second option, *Start New Procedure*, instead. It won't do a lot – all you will see is the screen go blank for a second or so and then the menu reappear with the highlight bar covering the third menu option. But behind the scenes DataEase has been very busy clearing room for your first bit of programming.

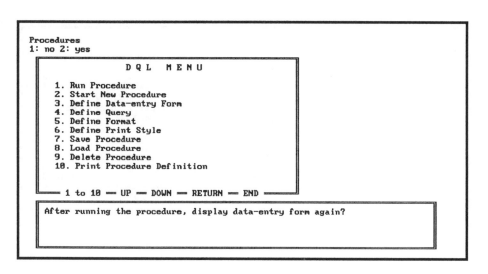

The Query Language Menu screen

Now select the option highlighted, *Define Data Entry Form*, by pressing either <Enter> or the number 3 on your keyboard. DataEase will now enquire whether, once the procedure has been run, you require the data entry form to be displayed again. Where data entry is concerned the answer will almost always be *Yes* as after one form has been completed you are likely to want to enter another. For example, it would be annoying to have to keep going back to the menu after entering some information (which would be the result if you answered *No* to this question) if you had a pile of forms to key.

So respond by pressing either Y or the number 2, as DataEase has indicated that it will treat the number 2 as a positive response at the head of the screen. You will now be presented with a blank screen upon which to design your data entry screen.

Designing these is as much fun as designing a form, with the added attraction that you can introduce colours into the scheme of things. I'll explain how to do that straightaway.

Position the cursor about halfway across the third line down from the top of the screen. Now type in the text *Porterhouse College Lecturer Record*. As you may have guessed we still have a few more lecturers to record upon our database and they are going to be entered via the data entry screen we are now designing.

Now it would be nice to have that title stand out from the rest of the screen display. This we can achieve by making it appear in a different colour. Position the cursor one character to the left of the word Porterhouse and then press <F4>. At the base of the screen you will have noticed the usual collection of Hot Keys and <F4> gives you access to a number of commands that appear in pop-down menus.

```
 Form:                        R  1 C  1
    Exit        Edit       Tools      Highlight
                                   ┌─────────────────────────────────────────┐
                                   │Show Colors                         Alt-S│
                                   │Underline   (Regular Field Color)   Alt-U│
                                   │Bold           (Highlight 1 Color)  Alt-B│
                                   │Italics        (Highlight 2 Color)  Alt-I│
                                   │CPI 2 (Title Area Color)                 │
                                   │CPI 3 (Mode Area Color)                  │
                                   │CPI 4 (Message Area Color)               │
                                   │LPI 2 (Prompt Line Color)                │
                                   │LPI 3 (Menu Highlight Color)             │
                                   │LPI 4 (Key Names Color)                  │
                                   │End Highlight                       Alt-E│
                                   └─────────────────────────────────────────┘




 F4CMDHELP ESCEXIT F2SAVE F3CUT F5COPY F6PASTE F7DELLN F8INSLN F10FIELD
```

The pop-down Colour control menu

<F4> has four such menus, each accessed by the use of the left and right cursor keys. I'll return to cover the other menus in a moment but just for now keep pressing the cursor key with the right pointing arrow until you reach the last menu list as it is displayed above.

This menu controls the colour and display of screen text during record entry. Alas it does not permit the colours used to display data to be changed – here you are forced to rely on the screen colours that DataEase's designers thought were best.

Here's a breakdown of the various menu options:

Show Colors

American spelling again! . . . but this option allows you to have a look at how your screen will appear when it is displayed during data entry. Any colours that have used will be shown. This does not happen during the screen's design stage, when, instead, you just get the attribute codes at the start and end of each highlighted area, which are not too meaningful until you get used to them.

You could, instead of pressing <F4> and then accessing this menu, just press <Alt> and <S> at the same time to get this effect.

Underline

This will cause the bit of text you highlight to be underlined and appear in the regular field colours as yellow text on a blue background. Press <Alt> and <U> to avoid having to use the <F4> menu route.

Bold

As it suggests this will make the text stand out, it will appear in the Highlight 1 colour mode which defaults to white text on a red background. Press <Alt> and <B> to achieve this effect directly.

Italic

Italic text will appear in the Highlight 2 colour mode of yellow text against a black background. To fast-key this attribute press <Alt> and <I>.

CPI 2/3/4 LPI 2/3/4

Unfortunately there is no fast-key way of applying these colour attributes which are described in the Table 3.1.

Table 3.1: Colour attributes – default values

CPI 2	Title area	Yellow text on a black background
3	Mode area	Cyan text on a black background
4	Message area	Red text on a black background
LPI 2	Prompt line	Black text on a green background
3	Menu highlight	White text on a blue background
4	Key names	White text on a red background

Note: All the above colour settings are the default values. These can be amended using the Define Screen Style menu function which is detailed later in this book.

Our title field is to appear as white text upon a red background so move the highlight bar with the cursor key marked with a downwards pointing arrow until it covers the LPI 4 Key Names Colour option then press <Enter> to select it.

DataEase will now return you to the text on the screen and the following prompt will appear on the screen:

Move cursor to end of <Highlight> and press Alt-E. Press Esc to cancel.

So move the cursor until it is one character to the right of the word Record and then press <Alt> and <E> together. You should now see the attribute control characters

@l4 and @l1 appear at each end of the title text. Now if you press <Alt> and <S> you will get a preview of how the screen will look when it is displayed – see one screen title nicely standing out from the rest of the screen. Press <Enter> to return to the data entry design screen.

You will already be familiar with some of the other commands on the pop-down menu screens accessed via <F4>, for example, the Exit commands we've met before and the Cut and Paste instructions. However, the third menu contains some instructions that are new to us so let's cover those quickly before moving on to finish the design of this data entry screen.

Field

As you will discover in a moment, the data entry screen can contain fields just like a form. This command, which can also be accessed directly by pressing <F10>, allows you to access and amend a fields properties. You should note, however, that such changes only apply to the data entry screen in question, they will not cascade down to any other places where that field is described, i.e other data entry screens or forms, but will remain unique to that data screen.

Borders & Ext Char Set

This command, that can also be accessed directly by pressing <Alt> and <F10>, allows you, among other things, to place borders around your screens or blocks of text. It will also let you form text characters from the IBM extended ANSI character set.

Unfortunately you will not get a chance to play with them while building the Porterhouse database but here's how to place, and remove, a border.

Before pressing <F4> and accessing the pop-down menus (or if you prefer pressing <Alt> and <F10>) position the cursor at the point on the screen where you wish the upper left-hand corner of the border to be drawn. Now press the required keys and the menu will appear offering you three border-related choices and a fourth regarding the IBM character set. Select either the Single or Double border option as required by moving the highlight bar until your selection is covered and then pressing <Enter>.

Then move the cursor down to where you wish the bottom right-hand corner to be drawn and then press <Alt> and <F10> to cause the border to be drawn. If <Esc> is pressed at any stage up to this point the Border instruction will be cancelled.

To delete a border, just position the cursor on the upper left-hand corner of the border and then press <Alt> and <F10>. Select Erase Border from the menu options.

Two points are worth remembering when drawing borders:

❏ Should a border be drawn over any text, that text will disappear from the screen

❏ If any part of a border line passes through a record entry field, that part of the line will not appear upon the screen. So take care!

Using a character from the IBM extended character set is just as straightforward. Position the cursor on the screen where you wish the character to be displayed, then press <Alt> and <F10) to access the pop-down menu. All you need to do then is select your character from those listed by DataEase and straightaway it will appear upon the screen. Once there, it can be treated just like any other character, i.e. it can be moved, copied or deleted as required.

Copy a Form – <F5>

That's enough about pop-down menus for the time being as we've still a little more work to do regarding the design of our data entry screen.

We've a nice title but something is missing from the screen. Of course, some fields need to be provided for our database user to enter information into! There are two ways of approaching this, the hard way or the lazy way. For you masochists out there, let's discuss the hard way for a few moments and then we can get on and do it the easy way.

Think about the purpose of this data entry screen. It is to provide a means of recording a lecturer's name and address details upon the database. Therefore it's fairly evident that the fields we described upon the Lecturer form will need to appear upon this screen. The hard way says that we must go through the agony of describing each of those fields again, something we've just completed during Chapter 2.

It is extremely important that, in order for our first bit of DQL programming to work, the fields on the data entry screen have exactly the same description applied to them as during form design. One extra character added to a field's length or a number described as a Numeric String rather than an Integer and our data entry system will be right up the creek. But if you really want to do it the hard way that's an indication of how much care and work is involved.

Fortunately for those of us who like to take life a bit easier the DataEase programmers felt the same way. So they went ahead and provided the <F5> option. We met this command in Chapter 2 and it has not really changed much as it can still be used to Copy a block of text around the screen. But at this point it is one of its other little tricks that interests us – its ability to copy Forms.

This key provides a means by which we can copy all the fields held on the Lecturer form onto this screen. No risk of getting a description wrong now! So I'll leave it up to you to decide how you want to get your screen to look something like the one pictured below . . . I know which way I did it. Don't forget to delete the Lecturer Number field from this screen.

Note the attribute characters used in the instruction line.

Hint: The characters appear as white on a blue background

```
 ┌────────────────────────────────────────────────────────────────────────┐
 │                                                                          │
 │   Form: RECORD LECTURER        R   1 C    1                              │
 │                                                                          │
 │                                                                          │
 │                    @14 << PORTERHOUSE COLLEGE LECTURER RECORD >> @11      │
 │   SURNAME                    CHRISTIAN NAMES                 TITLE     AGE│
 │                   HOME ADDRESS                                            │
 │                                                                          │
 │                                                                          │
 │   POST CODE                                TELEPHONE NUMBER              │
 │   DATE EMPLOYED                                                          │
 │   SALARY                                   PREVIOUS POST                 │
 │                                                                          │
 │   PRESS @13<ESC@11> TO EXIT OR COMPLETE FORM BEFORE PRESSING @13<F2>@11 TO UPDATE│
 │   DATABASE                                                               │
 │                                                                          │
 │  F4CMDHELP ESCEXIT F2SAVE F3CUT F5COPY F6PASTE F7DELLN F8INSLN F10FIELD   │
 └────────────────────────────────────────────────────────────────────────┘
```

The Lecturer Data Entry screen

Now if you remember when we defined the fields upon the Lecturer form none of them was flagged as being Required. This now has to be addressed, as while not every address line might be required, details such as a name must be keyed.

We can achieve this very easily by moving the cursor until it is somewhere within a field's area and then pressing <F10>. As a result the field definition screen will appear enabling us to amend that field's characteristics. The only fields that don't need to be marked as Required are Home Address Lines 3 and 4, Home Tel Code and Home Tel No. So please <F10> all the other fields marking them as Required.

This is another advantage of using this method of data entry, as each data entry form can have its own unique Required field criteria independently of the Form itself. Any field amendments made upon a data entry form are NOT reflected upon their owner Form.

To complete the data entry form we need to add some instructions for our user to follow. Although we have an idea what the Hot Key prompts at the base of the screen are used for, it is unlikely that our user will. So let's be as user friendly as DataEase. This is accomplished by adding some background text onto the screen that reads:

Press <Esc> to exit or complete form before pressing <F2> to update database

In order for the user easily to identify the keys that need to be pressed it is a good idea to make them stand out from the rest of the text by highlighting them, just as we did earlier with the title text. So here is another opportunity for you to practise using colours.

Position the cursor over the < before Esc, and then press <F4>, move across to the last menu screen and then select *LPI 3 Menu Highlight Colour* from the schemes provided. DataEase will now return you to the screen, so you can continue by moving the cursor until it covers the > immediately after Esc. Now press <Alt> and <E> together and you should be rewarded by seeing the attribute control characters popping into view either side of the characters <Esc>. Now do the same for <F2>.

Don't worry about the screen message wrapping around the screen to take up two lines. The attribute control characters are *invisible* when the screen is actually displayed, and DataEase happily ignores the room they take up on the line, displaying the message as if they did not exist. Press <Alt> and <S> at the same time to prove this to yourself.

Fine, that's our first data entry form completed, so now save it by pressing <F2>. This action stores the data entry form upon DataEase, where, incidentally, it is considered to be no different from any other form created using the Form Definition menu. This means that it can be referred to in Relationships, which opens up whole new avenues for us to explore later.

And as with those forms, you can return to amend this screen if you wish. Should you do so, DataEase will demand some information from you first before displaying the screen for amendment. Its initial question will ask if the existing data entry screen is to be deleted – respond as required. Next DataEase will want to know if it is to redisplay the screen after data has been recorded – again answer as the situation demands.

Now take a deep breath, because the time has finally arrived for us to have a go at a bit of computer programming. Select option 4, *Define Query*, from the menu and enter the world of DQL (DataEase Query Language).

DataEase Query Language

You should now be looking at a fairly blank screen. Across its base is the usual selection of Hot Key commands, while near the top is a line displaying the names of our Forms. Above that, written in white text upon a red background, is a prompt urging us to *Select Form name* and finally, there is the word *For* followed by a flashing white line, displayed a little way down the screen. This is where the work area starts, within which, we are going to construct our DQL commands.

The authors of DataEase have carried the user-friendly concept almost to its extremes with regard to writing DQL code. You don't literally have to spell out a single word or phrase. Instead, every command that DataEase will understand can be accessed via Choice lists. What is more, the program is intelligent enough just to provide those commands that logically follow the previous command it received. It almost writes the DQL instructions itself and all you have to do is press the right buttons at the right time.

So relax and then start by pressing one of the Hot Keys, namely the one marked <F9>. You'll notice that is has the text Query Level Low associated with it, or if you've already pressed that key the Low has been replaced with High. This key simply controls the amount of assistance DataEase will provide when you are programming DQL code. As this is our first attempt at writing some code we'd appreciate all the help we can get, but as you get more experienced DataEase advice can become a little irritating, hence the thoughtful provision of a Low setting to reduce DataEase's affability.

Having set that flag to High our next step will be to delete the word *For*. This is one of DataEase's most powerful commands, one that will make good use of later, but it is not required at this moment. So remove it from the screen using <Delete>.

To access DataEase's command list you need only press <F1>. The list of Form names at the top of the screen will now be replaced by a Choice menu detailing a few of the command words. Press <F1> again, and more will be displayed inside a column down the right-hand side of the screen. DataEase indicates that more are available by showing that 35 commands exist and that the others can be accessed by pressing <PgDn>. But stick with those already displayed just for now.

Let's pause for a moment to consider what we want DataEase to do for us. Some information is going to be keyed onto the Data Entry screen we've just finished designing and we wish that data to be entered onto the database. Look down the list of commands provided and try to spot which seems most likely to do that action for us.

The command Enter a Record looks like a winner to me. The others available will be discussed as we come to use them. So let's continue on by selecting that command and DataEase will display it as the first line in our work area.

Because DataEase knows that that command relates to a Form, it now helpfully displays the names of all our Forms back on the screen, so that we can indicate which one is to receive the information that's been keyed. In this case its the Lecturer form, so select that from the list and DataEase will add its name to the end of our first DQL instruction. This should now read:

```
ENTER A RECORD IN Lecturer
```

The cursor will also have moved down a line ready for our next code instruction. Again DataEase is eager to help, suggesting that we now select the Lecturer Form fields into which data is to be placed.

Select Surname and that title will appear upon the screen followed by the characters :=. This is DataEase's equals sign. It now prompts us for the value the field named Surname on the Lecturer form is to be given by displaying three choices, namely 0 = None, 1 = Current and 2 = Data-entry.

0 = None Not what it might suggest. This is simply a means of indicating that you wish a field to have a value other than those indicated. Usually in response to pressing the Zero button you will be invited to provide a default value for the field in question.

1 = Current Current Functions such as Current Time and Date were covered in Chapter 2. This is a means by which a field can be allocated a current function value.

2 = Data-entry Via this option it is possible to link a field's value to that provided upon the data entry form.

As we want to link the Lecturer form field Surname to a data entry field, it is option 2 that we need to select. In return, DataEase will provide a list of the fields displayed upon the data entry screen, allowing us to choose the Surname field as the one required. Do you see now why it is good practice to maintain the same field names as much as is possible? It makes DQL programming simple. So now the second line of code should read:

```
SURNAME := data-entry SURNAME
```

DataEase now wants to know if any other fields are to be linked. The answer is to be yes, so it will once again display the list of Lecturer form fields from which we can select the next field to be updated. Follow the same procedure as above for every field on the form, save the Lecturer Number field, which we'll discuss in a moment, until no more are available, then answer No to DataEase's enquiry whether more fields are to be linked.

The final code should look like this:

```
ENTER A RECORD IN Lecturer
    SURNAME              := data-entry SURNAME;
    CHRISTIAN NAMES      := data-entry CHRISTIAN NAMES;
    TITLE                := data-entry TITLE;
    AGE                  := data-entry AGE;
    HOME ADDRESS LINE 1  := data-entry HOME ADDRESS LINE 1;
    HOME ADDRESS LINE 2  := data-entry HOME ADDRESS LINE 2;
    HOME ADDRESS LINE 3  := data-entry HOME ADDRESS LINE 3;
```

```
HOME ADDRESS LINE 4 := data-entry HOME ADDRESS LINE 4;
HOME POSTCODE        := data-entry HOME POSTCODE;
HOME TEL CODE        := data-entry HOME TEL CODE;
HOME TEL NO          := data-entry HOME TEL NO;
PREVIOUS POST        := data-entry PREVIOUS POST;
SALARY               := data-entry SALARY;
DATE EMPLOYED        := data-entry DATE EMPLOYED.
```

And that's it done! That's a complete DQL procedure all written and ready to run. Go on, congratulate yourself for a few moments, you deserve it.

Of course, it is possible to make them far more involved than this but the basic concept of menu selecting commands and form/field names remains consistent throughout.

The procedure as it now stands will work and can be saved using the utilitarian <F2> key. However, there is another, quicker way that we could have written the above code that would have saved us a lot of key pressing. It is a method that can only be used when every data entry field name and description exactly matches the Form field into which its data is to be passed. Providing that criteria is satisfied, this short cut can be used. This is where I get mean, having just had you do all that work keying the DQL code in, I now want you to delete it all, leaving only the line:

`ENTER A RECORD IN Lecturer`

Stop abusing this book and get on with it!. All done? Good. Now press <F1> to have all the field names redisplayed at the top of the screen and then select option 0 (None). In response DataEase will invite you to make one of two choices: 0 (None) that will result in all the field names being displayed again, or 1 <Copy All From>.

Guess which one we are going to use!

DataEase will now offer two possible places from which data can be copied from: Current Functions or Data-Entry. On this occasion we need to opt for Data-Entry. The commands will now read:

```
ENTER A RECORD IN Lecturer
COPY ALL FROM data-entry
```

Much shorter and much less effort than having to pair up lots of fields names, and just as effective. Again <F2> will save this code onto DataEase. Incidentally, DataEase will not object if you prefer to type in these commands directly rather than using the choice-driven facility. I tend to use a bit of both, depending upon how I feel and how complex the procedure is that I am building.

You might be wondering about the Lecturer Number field. Well if you recall, this was set up as a Sequence field. Accordingly, DataEase will automatically calculate a value for this field without us having to do a single thing. Why can't life always be that easy?

Run Procedure

Having returned to the DQL menu, now select option 7, *Save Procedure*. A prompt will appear near the bottom of the screen requesting that you provide a name for the procedure. As the title Record Lecturer seems appropriate, type that and DataEase will store away your DQL code.

I suppose you now want to find out how well your code works? Okay, select option 1 from the DQL menu list to start your procedure running.

Immediately you will be presented with the Data Entry screen that you designed. Type in the information below and then follow your own instructions by pressing <F2> to update the database.

Mr Richard Clancy   Age 50 Telephone (0271) 587431

                                     22 The Dorkings
                                     Harford Heath
                                     Hants
                                     HH3 HQ1
                                     Salary £70,000 Started 5th October 1982

                                     Previous Post Dorchester

The screen will blink, as DataEase saves the information, and then reappear blank, ready for the final lecturer's details to be keyed.

Sir James Leighton   Age 55 Telephone (0271) 585858

                                     The Priory
                                     Aversham Park
                                     Lower Stonely
                                     Hants
                                     AP1 H15
                                     Salary £80,000 Started 16th May 1972

                                     Previous Post None

Once you've keyed this information, return to the Main menu and select option 2, *Record Entry*. No we are not going to add any more data just yet, but this provides a quick means by which you can reassure yourself that the data you've just supplied has been recorded upon the database.

Follow the same steps as described at the start of this chapter, access the Lecturer form and then view its Form Records in tabular form by pressing <Shift> and <F1> at the same time. The two lecturers named above should have their details displayed at the bottom of the table.

Remaining Data Entry

Together we've now covered the three different methods of recording data upon our DataEase database. The first two are primarily used by the database designer/ administrator and the third by other users of the database.

As the Porterhouse database steadily gets built, more data will need to be keyed into it. I'll leave it up to you to decide which method of data entry you employ but I would suggest you design at least one other data entry screen and DQL procedure.

So before leaving this chapter, the information displayed below needs to be input into the database. The report was produced by DataEase and an explanation of the technique involved will be discussed in the next chapter.

```
LIST COURSES                          Running report LIST COURSES
END OF REPORT. SPACE: Return to Menu   PgUp: Scroll

                    PORTERHOUSE CURRICULUM

        ===================================================
              COURSE            COURSE              COURSE
              NUMBER             TITLE               FEE
        ---------------------------------------------------
                001      ADVANCED ENGINEERING        50.00
                002      BASIC COMPUTER SKILLS       35.00
                003      ADVANCED SOCIAL SCIENCES    40.00
                004      ENGLISH LITERATURE          40.00
                005      PHYSICAL EDUCATION          25.00
        ===================================================
```

The courses available at Porterhouse

The following nine students also need to have their data recorded. Note that the Date Enrolled field does not need to be displayed upon the data entry form as we can get DataEase to calculate it for us. The DQL required to do this will read:

```
ENTER A RECORD IN STUDENT
COPY ALL FROM data-entry;
DATE ENROLLED := CURRENT DATE
```

Mrs Elizabeth Smith   Age 30 + Employment = Business

Home   11 Orwell Court
                             Hurricane Way
                             Puddlesbridge
                             Hants
                             HH2 5GW   Telephone 0271-455221

Work   Masterkey Systems
                             37 Westface Road
                             Gt Lincolns
                             Hants
                             H13 4FF   Telephone 0271-224556

                             Contacted = Mailshot   Enrolment Fee £25.00

Mr Ian Pendlebury   Age 21+   Employment = Unemployed

Home   12 Duke Street
                             Lower Stanbury
                             Hants
                             HS1 HB2

                             Contacted = Mailshot Enrolment Fee £10.00

Mr Andrew Jerman   Age 40+   Employment = Self Employed

Home   3 Derby Street
                             Hamlet
                             Hants
                             HH3 2QW   Telephone 0271-778120

Work   36 Clarence Street
                             High Locum
                             Hants   Telephone 0271-905825

                             Contacted = Local Paper   Enrolment Fee £25.00

Mr Edward Dyer   Age 40+   Employment = Business

Home   8 Galliford Way
                                  Westbury
                                  Hants
                                  HW1 2XF

Work   TTD Transport
                                  1 Alicia Way
                                  Westbury
                                  Hants   Telephone 0271-447844

                                  Contacted Word of Mouth   Enrolment Fee £25.00

Miss Angela Rogers   Age 18+   Employment = Student

Home   111 Tudor Road
                                  Clydons
                                  Hants
                                  HC5 7YY   Telephone 0271-556907

                                  Contacted Radio Advert   Enrolment fee £10.00

Mrs Mary Alexander   Age 30+   Employment = Other

Home   2 St Johns Walk
                                  Dunmow
                                  Hants
                                  HD4 5TH   Telephone 0271-556201

                                  Contacted Word of Mouth   Enrolment Fee £10.00

Mr Chris James   Age 55+   Employment = Business
Home   23 Clifftown Way
                                  Clifftown
                                  Hants
                                  HC4 5RR   Telephone 0271-213111

Work   Globe House
                                  211 Chursty Avenue
                                  Clifftown

Hants
HC4 4FG   Telephone 0271-224475 ext 2156

Contacted = Local Paper   Enrolment fee £25.00

Mrs Fiona James   Age 55+   Employment = Others

Home   23 Clifftown Way
                              Clifftown
                              Hants
                              HC4 5RR   Telephone 0271-213111

                              Contacted Word o f Mouth   Enrolment fee £25.00

Mr Frank Adamson   Age 40+   Employment=Self Employed

Home   214 Brunton Avenue
                              Lower Stansford
                              Hants
                              HL2 3ER   Telephone 0271-447832

Work   21 The Arches
                              Lower Stansford
                              Hants
                              HL2 3ER   Telephone 0271-447925

                              Contacted = Mailshot   Enrolment fee £25.00

Simple Data Retrieval

If all you ever wanted to do was store some information upon a database, to all intents and purposes you could stop reading this book now. The data entry techniques described in Chapter 3 are all you ever need to know. However, I suspect, that some day, you will want to retrieve the data you've so carefully hoarded away. This chapter describes exactly how to do just that.

You've already had some experience of data retrieval. The data entry table discussed a few pages back not only provided a quick method of data entry, it also allowed you to see information already recorded upon the database. This could be described as *indirect* data retrieval as the information was unearthed while we were using the table for a different purpose. Within DataEase there are other such indirect methods of data access which I'll disclose later in this chapter.

For such experts as ourselves, indirect data retrieval techniques are fine, but what about any other users of the database. How are they to fare?

No problem, DataEase caters for them as well by providing a number of direct data access methods. One involves the use of DQL while the other requires no programming code to be written at all. I've a feeling that this second method is the one you'd prefer to cover first . . .

QBE – Quick Reports

Return to the Main menu screen by pressing the <Esc> key a few times and then select option 3, *Query by Example – Quick Reports*, from the choices of action displayed. This will cause the QBE Menu screen to be displayed.

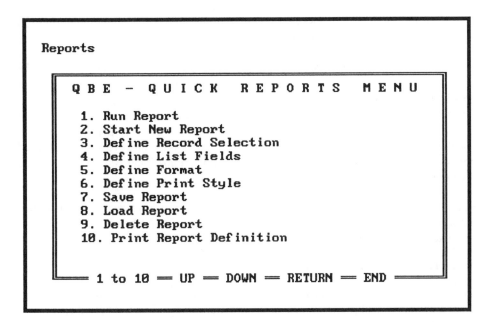

The QBE Menu screen

Don't get too perturbed if at first glance it looks exactly the same as the DQL menu you met in the previous chapter. Have another look and you will spot some subtle differences made to the options wording. The actions offered by this menu provide a straightforward means of data retrieval. They enable you quickly to set up information displays and reports without needing any DQL know how at all.

As with the DQL menu, ignore option 1, *Run Report*, and instead select the second option, *Start New Report*. The screen will flicker for a second and then the words *New Report Started* will appear in the top left-hand corner of the screen. DataEase is now ready for us to start to describe the data retrieval actions we wish it to perform.

The third menu option looks inviting but we are going to by-pass that for the moment and instead choose option 4, *Define List Fields*. You could, perhaps, argue a bit about the description used for this option, particularly as the next thing DataEase asks you to do is to indicate which Form you are interested in, but it will begin to seem more sensible once we've progressed through the enquiry.

As you've just spent a lot of effort (I hope) in keying in the student's names and addresses let's realise an immediate reward by having DataEase display some of those details, plus the student's ID code (Student Number) in a report for us. Begin by choosing the Student form from those listed.

A screen, uncannily like the Student form description should now appear upon your screen. Consider the information that you wish to obtain. As this is our first report let's keep things simple by just requesting students' names, home addresses and I.D codes. This we can communicate to DataEase quite easily.

Position the cursor somewhere inside each of those fields in turn, and then press the spacebar. As each field is selected you will see a number appear against it. This details the order in which the fields will be displayed. So be sure to have the address fields numbered in sequence, otherwise the student's address information will be split all over the display screen/report. I am using the terms screen/report for a reason. DataEase can provide information in a number of formats, and we've already used one, namely the screen display. Others include print reports and files. These will be discussed in detail later in the book.

Returning to our field selection, it will probably have not have escaped your notice that as each field was chosen DataEase prompted you for further information about how each field was to be displayed. The wording:

Order, Reverse, Group, Sum, Count, Mean, Max, Min

appears at the top of the screen. It is quite in order for you to ignore them totally. They are simply display control properties and DataEase will happily produce a report for you without them.

Sometimes, however, they can be very useful. For example, in this case we might like the students to be listed in alphabetical order, or perhaps by ID Code. In which case the Order property becomes very useful.

```
Select Fields                    R  8 C  59
Press Space to mark field. Specify order reverse group count sum mean max or min

SURNAME  1 ORDER        CHRISTIAN NAMES  2              TITLE        AGE

HOME ADDRESS   3                         TELEPHONE NUMBER
               4
               5                         DATE ENROLED
               6
                                         STUDENT NUMBER    7 ORDER

POST CODE

WORK ADDRESS                             TELEPHONE NUMBER

                                         CONTACTED

                                         EMPLOYMENT

POST CODE                                ENROLLMENT FEE

COURSE FEES                              TOTAL CHARGED

F4CMDHELP ESCEXIT F2SAVE F5FORM CLR F6FLD CLR F1ØMULTI
```

The Student QBE enquiry form

All that is required, as you can see from the form above, is to type in the word *Order* against the field(s) you wish to have the information sorted upon. Any number of fields can be allocated the Order property, their importance in the sort being determined by their display sequence number.

For example, we've two students named James recorded upon our database. Were we simply to ask for the Surname field to be used to determine the display order of the Student information we could never be sure whose details would appear first, Mrs or Mr James. It's not particularly important for this report but it may be so for others.

Accordingly by setting the student ID Code as the second Order field we can be sure that the surnames will always be displayed in the order they were keyed onto the database: Mr James' details will always appear before Mrs James'. Incidentally, don't be concerned if there does not appear to be enough room to type a property's name into a field, i.e Order into a two character field, as DataEase will temporarily extend the field's size to accommodate whatever display information you want to provide.

Order

Determines the order in which fields are to be sorted

Reverse

Causes fields to be sorted in reverse order, i.e displayed in the order Z to A rather than A to Z.

Group

This property will cause all like fields to be grouped in the report. For example, were this property to be applied to the Surname field (and no other fields be allocated display properties) the following report would result:

```
SURNAME
----------------

ADAMSON
ALEXANDER
DYER
JAMES

JERMAN
PENDLEBURY
ROGERS
SMITH
```

Not too useful on this occasion as all it does is list out the Surnames recorded but it can be used to good effect, particularly inside DQL written procedures. When you come to use Define Format (QBE Menu option 5) and the use of Groups has been requested, DataEase will enquire if you wish Group Headers and Trailers to be provided (Chapter 6 provides more details). These can be very desirable, especially if numeric fields have been grouped in which case a total figure can be obtained.

In the above example, however, the only result of replying Yes would be to have the information supplied slightly differently.

```
SURNAME    ADAMSON
SURNAME    ALEXANDER
SURNAME    DYER
SURNAME    JAMES
SURNAME    JERMAN
SURNAME    PENDLEBURY
SURNAME    ROGERS
SURNAME    SMITH
```

In the first example, the gap between James and Jerman is deliberate, this being one of the ways DataEase indicates that a group item occurs more than once.

Sum

Provides the sum total of a number of numeric fields added together. If the field named Enrolment Fee were to be given this property, all the fees paid would be listed plus a total figure, in this case £180.00.

Count

As the name suggests this property causes a counter to be created, that will automatically be incremented each time the associated field is encountered. To demonstrate its purpose let's consider the Student ID Code (Student Number) field. Surely its latest value also reflects the number of students presently attending the college. Well maybe, maybe not. The Student Number field is calculated in sequence, based upon the latest number issued, and not how many student forms exist, therefore it cannot be relied upon to provide this information accurately. At best it can only reveal how many students have attended the college in total, not how many are enrolled at the moment.

But apply the Count property to this field and DataEase will return an accurate count of how many students the college is educating.

Mean

For Mean read Average. DataEase will compute the average value for a field's contents. Using this property the average Enrolment Fee can be determined to be £20.00.

```
STUDENT ADDRESSES              Running report STUDENT ADDRESSES
END OF REPORT. SPACE: Return to Menu    PgUp Home LEFT RIGHT Arrows: Scroll

=========================================================================
    SURNAME      CHRISTIAN    HOME ADDRESS LINE   HOME ADDRESS LINE   HOME ADD
                 NAMES               1                   2

-------------------------------------------------------------------------
    ADAMSON      FRANK        214 BRUNTON AVENUE  LOWER STANSFORD     HANTS
    ALEXANDER    MARY         2 ST JOHNS WALK     DUNMOW              HANTS
    DYER         EDWARD       8 GALLIFORD WAY     WESTBURY            HANTS
    JAMES        CHRIS        23 CLIFFTOWN WAY    CLIFFTOWN           HANTS
    JAMES        FIONA        23 CLIFFTOWN WAY    CLIFFTOWN           HANTS
    JERMAN       ANDREW       3 DERBY STREET      HAMLET              HANTS
    PENDLEBURY   LESTER IAN   12 DUKE STREET      LOWER STANBURY      HANTS
    ROGERS       ANGELA       111 TUDOR ROAD      CLYDONS             HANTS
    SMITH        ELIZABETH    11 ORWELL COURT     HURRICANE WAY       PUDDLESBR
=========================================================================
```

An example of a columnar format report

Max

Max is the highest value found for a field. So, if applied to the Enrolment Fee field this would result in a value of £25.00.

Min

Min is the lowest value found for a field. The lowest Enrolment Fee field value would be reported as £10.00.

Run Procedure

Having indicated the fields that you are interested in, and the order in which they are to be displayed now press <F2> to return to the menu screen. It is important to note that were you to select no fields at all from those offered, DataEase would assume that you wished ALL the fields upon the chosen form to be displayed.

First save the procedure, by pressing key <7> and then naming it Student Addresses, before pressing key <1> to select the first menu option, *Run Procedure*. After a very brief delay, DataEase will display a screen showing the information that was requested. See how it details every student we have recorded upon the database, not just one. Note also that the last two address columns and the student number are not displayed. This is simply because there is not enough room upon the screen to detail all the information at the same time. Press the right arrow key and this information will be displayed.

DataEase appreciates that this might not be the way that you wish the information to be displayed. Hence the provision of option 5, Define Format, which is discussed in detail in Chapter 6. But here's a sneak preview of some of the things it will help you to do.

```
1: no 2: yes

        Minimum line length for a columnar report is 119
        What type of report format do you want? : Columnar
        What line length do you desire for the report?  :  80
        report must be edited to fit into this line length! OK? :
```

The Display Format Definition screen

First select that menu option. DataEase will respond by displaying the screen on the previous page.

The statement on the first line reading:

Minimum length for a columnar report is 119

is purely informational. It is simply telling you how many columns across the screen or print are required to provide the report. Although printer paper can come in many sizes, bear in mind that you are restricted to a maximum of 80 columns across your computer screen when reading this information.

On the next line you are asked:

What type of report do you want?

DataEase suggests the default display format of columnar. For the moment we'll accept its advice and continue on by pressing <Enter>. In return we'll now be asked another question:

What line length do you desire for the report?

and again DataEase provides a suggested response of 80 columns. If, as in this case, the report is to be displayed upon the screen, the default figure can be left to stand. However, were the report to be produced as printer output, consideration should be given to the width of the paper being used. If sufficient room is available to print 119 columns in a single row, let DataEase know this by changing this figure from 80 to 119.

If you are stuck with a report requiring more columns than are available, don't worry. As you've already seen, DataEase copes with large screen displays by breaking up the report into screen sections. Print reports, unfortunately, cannot be so tidily dealt with. While DataEase will still provide all the information requested, it will appear on more than one print line, causing a rather messy looking output. Chapter 6 will detail ways of circumventing this problem.

At this stage let us again take DataEase's advice, by remaining with a line length of 80 characters, and press the <Enter> key once more to continue. As if to rebuff us for being so foolish as to place trust in its counselling DataEase now immediately warns us:

`Report must be edited to fit into this line length.`

Having proved its superiority to its own satisfaction it will now calmly await our response. This can either be Yes – meaning we know but don't care, or No – that's the last time we trust you mate!

The program will accept either response, a No causing a return to the *What line length do you want?* prompt. As we've gone this far, and know that DataEase will cough up all the information we want anyway, it makes sense to respond with a positive answer.

DataEase will then proceed to display a screen that shows how it will lay out the information. This can be edited and field positions moved, however, you'll have to be patient for now, as the necessary techniques are not discussed until Chapter 6. So, press <F2> to return to the QBE menu screen, then once again press <1> to re-run the procedure.

Lo and behold, you see exactly the same information screen as before . . . which is not too surprising as all we have done is accept DataEase's default display format values. Let's change that cosy arrangement right now.

Return to the Define Format screen (Menu option <5>) where you will find a different message waiting. As we've already defined a report format, DataEase is somewhat miffed that we now want to change our minds and wants us to reconsider this decision, craftily wording a leading question:

`Do you wish to keep the existing format?`

If you were to answer Yes, a distinctly pleased program would return you to the QBE menu screen. However, let us continue irritating it by replying No – we want to change the report's format.

Somewhat disappointingly the computer will not erupt into flames at this point. Instead it will calmly respond by telling us the number of columns within which it can display the report in a columnar format. No doubt, it is still hoping to persuade us that this is really the best path to follow. You can now disappoint it further by pressing <2> – thus selecting the *Field by Line* report format instead. As per DataEase standard the various report formats available will be listed as Choice options across the top of the screen. The <F1> key, as ever, signifies that more choices are available.

Accepting the inevitable, DataEase will now show you what the new display will look like. Press <F2> to accept the display, and then <1>, *Run Report*, to view the screen report.

```
STUDENT ADDRESSES                              Running procedure STUDENT ADDRESSES
SPACE or PgDn: More   EXIT: Abort PgUp Home LEFT RIGHT Arrows: Scroll
================================================================================
    SURNAME                                ADAMSON
    CHRISTIAN NAMES                        FRANK
    HOME ADDRESS LINE 1                    214 BRUNTON AVENUE
    HOME ADDRESS LINE 2                    LOWER STANSFORD
    HOME ADDRESS LINE 3                    HANTS
    HOME ADDRESS LINE 4
    STUDENT NUMBER                         0008

    SURNAME                                ALEXANDER
    CHRISTIAN NAMES                        MARY
    HOME ADDRESS LINE 1                    2 ST JOHNS WALK
    HOME ADDRESS LINE 2                    DUNMOW
    HOME ADDRESS LINE 3                    HANTS
    HOME ADDRESS LINE 4
    STUDENT NUMBER                         0006

    SURNAME                                DYER
    CHRISTIAN NAMES                        EDWARD
    HOME ADDRESS LINE 1                    8 GALLIFORD WAY
    HOME ADDRESS LINE 2                    WESTBURY
```

An example of a field by line format display

The processing options offered by the QBE – Quick Reports Menu provided a gentle introduction into the art of Data Retrieval Techniques. QBEs are generally used to produce quick, off the cuff, reports. In order to furnish more detailed information you are usually required to make use of the DQL language. You've already had a little play at programming, so now it's time to start getting your hands dirty.

Return to the Main menu screen and then select option 4, *DQL Advanced Processing.*

DQL Data Retrieval Techniques

To date the Porterhouse database has had three types of information recorded upon it, namely the names and addresses of its lecturers, the courses it runs, and name/address data relating to the students. Using QBE, a report holding the students' home addresses information was produced, so now, via DQL, let us write a procedure to list the courses available at the college.

First press <2>, *Start New Procedure*, to clear an area within DataEase to write the code. Once the DQL menu screen has been re-established select option 4, *Define Query*. You should now be looking at the DQL work area form familiar from Chapter 3, with the key word *For* already displayed upon the screen.

As with data entry, DataEase makes life easy for us with data retrieval. Listed along the top of the screen are the names of our forms, ready for us to choose one. Select the one named Course. Our work area on the screen should now read:

`For COURSE`

The top of the screen will have changed as well. Instead of the form names, the strange wording *0: None 1: With* has appeared. To understand what DataEase is asking we need first to translate into English the DQL code we've so far written. Basically it states:

For every Form named Course, that has information recorded upon it

DataEase now wants to know if we want to apply any further conditions to that statement. For example, if we wanted the report to detail only those courses with 30 students we would need to add the wording:

With Actual Number of Students = 30.

As, in this case, we want every form to be reported regardless of its class size, our response to the question is to press <0> – None, meaning no further conditions are required. This response causes DataEase to add some further code onto the screen, namely a line containing a single semi-colon ; and then immediately below the wording . . . *List records.*

```
For COURSE
;
list records
```

Translated, this means:

For every Form named Course, that has information recorded upon it, produce a report.

At the top of the screen DataEase has helpfully listed some of the names of the fields held upon the Course form. Others, of course, are available by pressing <F1>. It now wants us to tell it which field values we are interested in. Being a simple report, we only require three field values to be shown, the first being the course's unique reference number, held in the field named Course Number. So select that field from those listed and its name will appear on the line below the wording *List records.*

DataEase will now prompt you to supply a display control property (Order, Group, Sum etc) to that field – remember we met some of these while building the QBE procedure. It seems sensible to request that the forms be sorted into Course Number order so select the property *In Order* from the list displayed. Our code should now read:

```
for COURSE
;
list records
   COURSE NUMBER in order
```

Finally you are asked:

Are any more fields to be listed?

Replying Yes causes DataEase, after it has first placed a semi-colon at the end of that line, to once again list the available field titles at the top of the screen. From these, select the Course Title field, so that the name of the course is reported. It is not necessary for that field to be a *sort key* so no display control property need be chosen. Instead, press <0> – None. Respond positively to DataEase's query regarding any more fields as one more, the Course Fee field, needs to be requested. As with the Course Title this, too, is not a sort field so reply accordingly.

You will next be prompted to reply to a question:

Any statistics desired on this item?

Ignore it, for now, by responding negatively. Its meaning and use will be covered in the next chapter. End by supplying a No answer to the question concerning more fields.

Somewhat disconcertingly the screen will now disappear, being replaced with the DQL menu screen. You haven't done anything wrong, neither have you lost your code. DataEase has simply got a bit above itself, by returning to the menu without giving you a chance to admire your code. Select option 4 once again and it will reappear on the screen, reading thus:

```
for COURSE
;
list records
   COURSE NUMBER in order ;
   COURSE TITLE ;
   COURSE FEE .
```

In English these commands read:

For every form named Course, that has information recorded upon it, produce a report. The forms are to be appear in course number order, detailing that number, the courses title and the cost of the course.

Having checked that everything is correct, press <F2> to return to the menu screen. As with the Data Entry code it is quite possible for you to write the above code by yourself independently of DataEase, which is only being user friendly. Just directly type and amend your programming instructions as you will.

Once back at the menu screen, save the procedure via option 7 naming it as *List Courses*, then give it a quick run via option 1 to see how it looks. Hopefully you will have something like the illustration, titled Porterhouse Curriculum that was shown in Chapter 3.

Having saved that procedure you will never have to write it again. Just load it up (select option 8 on the DQL menu list and then choose the procedure from those listed by DataEase) and then start it running.

DataEase writes its own procedures in exactly the same way. To prove this, load the QBE procedure Student Addresses using option 8 from the DQL menu. Before loading the code DataEase will display a message that reads:

Convert this QBE code (Quick Report) into a DQL procedure?

You will need to reply Yes in order to have the program loaded. Then using option 4, *Define Query*, take a look at DataEase's own code. It will appear very similar to the one you've just written.

This is because both these procedures were straightforward, simple interrogations of the database. DQL procedures can become far more complex as you will find out in Chapter 5. In the meantime how do you feel about programming now? Hopefully you are finding it a bit easier than you thought it would be.

Play around with DQL as much as you like. Follow DataEase's prompts and you'll always write code that works . . . whether or not it does what you want it to is another matter. That's something every computer programmer comes up against from time to time. Don't be afraid to experiment. As long as you are only reading (Listing) information you cannot do any harm to your database. It is only when you come to use commands like Delete and Amend that any real damage can occur.

If you are feeling confident, have a go at writing the List Lecturers procedure by yourself. Here's the specification for the report that is to list the lecturers' names and addresses in the order they were appointed to the college.

Form	LECTURER

Field order	TITLE
	CHRISTIAN NAMES
	SURNAME
	AGE
	HOME ADDRESS LINE 1
	HOME ADDRESS LINE 2
	HOME ADDRESS LINE 3
	HOME ADDRESS LINE 4
	HOME POSTCODE
	HOME TEL CODE
	HOME TEL NO
	LECTURER NUMBER
	SALARY
	DATE EMPLOYED

Key field	DATE EMPLOYED

If you need to cheat or just wish to confirm your code is correct, here's how it should appear:

```
for LECTURER
;
list records
   TITLE;
   CHRISTIAN NAMES;
   SURNAME;
   AGE;
   HOME ADDRESS LINE 1;
   HOME ADDRESS LINE 2;
   HOME ADDRESS LINE 3;
   HOME ADDRESS LINE 4;
   HOME POSTCODE;
   HOME TEL CODE;
   HOME TEL NO;
   LECTURER NUMBER;
   SALARY;
   DATE EMPLOYED in order.
```

Indirect Data Retrieval

Earlier mention was made of *indirect* data retrieval techniques such as occurred during table data entry. Another way of accessing data is provided via the Records menu which is entered using option 2, *Record Entry*, on the Main Menu.

This will cause the names of all the forms to be listed. Select the one in which you are interested, say the Lecturer form. DataEase will now display a blank Lecturer form for your use. Now, as explained earlier this can be used to enter information onto the database. But it can also be used to provide search instructions to DataEase, describing the record you want it to find.

To demonstrate this, let's assume you wish to access Dr Bishop's details. There are two ways this could be achieved: you keep pressing the Hot Key <F3> until the record you are interested in appears, or you supply DataEase with some search criteria and have it do all the work for you. Once your database has been in use for some time the first option could result in a blunt, and very sore, finger so my advice would be to get to know the second method.

It's very straightforward, requiring simply that you provide some information unique to the record you wish to access before starting the search off by pressing <F3>. In this case typing the doctor's christian and surname details should suffice. Once done, press <F3> and the good doctor's data will be displayed upon the screen. You can then amend or delete the record as you require. This can be a very useful facility when housekeeping (tidying up) your database.

5

Advanced DQL Retrieval

Over the previous two chapters you have been introduced to the DQL language used by DataEase, using it to both store and retrieve information from the database. The aim of this chapter is to help you to consolidate that knowledge while learning some advanced uses for the language. If all that sounds rather formidable, relax and think back to Chapter 2, when you were just a rookie database programmer. Now (if you've not skipped the exercises) you can justifiable claim to have advanced well beyond that stage. With a number of QBE and DQL programs behind you – who could call you a Rookie?

DQL can be used for many different purposes other than just data entry and retrieval. The language allows you do almost anything, even to the extent of permitting you to use another program, while still inside DataEase. For example, your database information could be transferred to a graphics program, where it can then be used to draw up a graph. Information from an outside program can even be passed back into DataEase for processing. These facilities make the DQL language a very powerful tool.

However, let's not try to fly too soon! The aim of this chapter, and indeed the book, is simply to get you up and running with DataEase. Once you've become fully confident with the program, you can start to dabble with its more exotic facilities. For now . . . well there's a little more information still to be recorded upon our Porterhouse database.

XRef Lecturer Course Procedure

We've identified the lecturers, students and the courses available at the college, but have yet to link either lecturer or student to any particular courses. Let's make a start by looking at a DQL procedure that will record which lecturer is responsible for which course.

This procedure will require two elements, namely the data-entry screen and the associated DQL code. First the screen: what information do we wish that to capture for us? Well, it will need to contain at least two important fields, one to identify the lecturer and another to distinguish the course. Now, it would quite reasonable for us to make use of the Course Title and Lecturer name fields for this purpose. However, were their information ever to be mistyped, it's possible your database could become corrupted. For example, should Mr Clancy's name be misspelt as Mr Clansea, data would be recorded upon the database for a mythical lecturer named Clansea, one unknown to you and the database, meaning that the error could only be recovered at the cost of some effort, once (if ever!) it has been found.

Better to avoid the possibility of a mistake right from the start by making use of the unique ID codes that were allocated to each course and lecturer. I am, of course, referring to the Lecturer Number and Course Number fields. The procedures List Courses and List Lecturers written in Chapter 4 will provide the means to identify the required numbers.

So, starting from the DQL menu screen, first select option 2, *Start New Procedure*, to clear a workarea inside DataEase, and then press <3>, *Define Data-Entry Form*. Next, move the cursor to about the middle of the screen before typing *Lecturer Course Allocation*, this being the screen's description. It's always a good idea to give each screen (Data Entry or Display) a title as it provides users with a point of reference should they ever need to ask for assistance.

```
Form: XREF LECTURER/COURSE
Press PgUp, PgDn, Home, or End to scroll. Press any other key to continue.


                    <<< LECTURER COURSE ALLOCATION >>>


        LECTURER NUMBER

        COURSE NUMBER


        First enter the Lecturer's I.D number and then the
        number of the course that they are to conduct.

             Press <F2> to update database

             or (ESC) to exit




 F4CMDHELP ESCEXIT F2SAVE F3CUT F5COPY F6PASTE F7DELLN F8INSLN F10FIELD
```

Lecturer Course allocation data-entry screen

The first field name, Lecturer Number, should now be typed upon the screen two lines below and to the left of title text. Next, move the cursor over a couple of columns, to leave a space, and then press <F10> to define the field's characteristics. All that is necessary here is to copy the field description that was given when defining the Lecturer Form, minus the derivation formula because that is not required here.

`LECTURER NUMBER    Numeric String    4 Digits    Formatted String = No`

Before pressing <F2> to save the description there is one more important thing to do. Set the Required field to Yes. This will ensure that a lecturer's number is always provided. We can now move down a further couple of lines and describe the Course Number field as follows:

`COURSE NUMBER    Numeric String`
`                 3 Digits Formatted String = No    Required = Yes`

We could leave our data-entry screen there. But in order to expand our growing expertise a bit further (and to be a bit flash) let's instruct DataEase to display automatically the lecturer's name and the course title upon the screen based upon the values keyed into the two fields we've just described. This will provide further insurance against mistakes, as the user can then be certain that they've typed in the right ID codes. It also gives us another opportunity to play with Relationships and the Lookup command.

Move the cursor back up to the line containing the Lecturer Number field. After leaving a small space, press F10 to access the field description form. As we neglected to provide a name for the field, DataEase has supplied one for us, namely Lecturer Number 2. Unfortunately, this is not the name we wish to use for this field as it is to display the Lecturer's title. So amend DataEase's suggested field name to read Title, before continuing on to describe the rest of the field.

`TITLE    CHOICE    Mr Mrs Ms Miss Dr Sir Lady`

Be very careful to ensure that the choice list values are in EXACTLY the same order as they are described on the Lecturer form, otherwise this procedure will fail to work properly. It's now time to call upon the Lookup command.

Move down to the Derivation area and then type this Lookup command:.

`LOOKUP "LECTURER NUM MATCH" TITLE`

We've yet to describe this Lecturer Num Match relationship – we'll do that once the DQL code has been written. Remember DataEase is not worried about when a Relationship is described, just as long as it has been, before any attempt is made to make use of it.

This code means, in Humanspeak:

Using the criteria laid down in the Lecturer Num Match relationship, locate the associated record and then copy the value of its Title field into this field.

In other words, find a Lecturer record with the same Lecturer number as that keyed into the Lecturer Number field on the screen and then display its Title upon the screen.

If you are still a little confused, don't worry, hopefully once all the bits have been put together, the Relationship, the data-entry screen and the DQL code, the picture will become much clearer. Finish off the field's description by setting Prevent Data Entry to Yes as we don't want any over keen user changing the lecturer's title. Finally, press <F2>, saving the field and return to the data-entry screen.

The cursor now has to be moved such that it lies just one column to the right of the end of the Title field's position. Here is where the lecturer's Christian names are to be displayed.

Press <F10> and commence to describe the field as:

```
CHRISTIAN NAMES    TEXT    14 characters
```

before once moving providing a derivation formula that should read:

```
LOOKUP "LECTURER NUM MATCH" "CHRISTIAN NAMES"

Prevent Data Entry = YES
```

It's the same relationship as above, but note the use of quotes around the field name Christian Names. Because this name consists of more than a single word DataEase requires that it be contained within quotes. If this is not done, DataEase will be unable to identify the required field correctly .

Save the field's description and return to describe the final field on this screen line, the Lecturer Surname. Position the cursor just off the end of the Christian Names field before pressing <F10. The field should be described thus:

```
SURNAME        TEXT    12 characters

Derivation Formula = LOOKUP "LECTURER NUM MATCH" SURNAME

Prevent Data Entry = YES
```

That leaves just one further field to be described. This being the Course Title, we need to position the cursor somewhere upon the same line as the Course Number field. Again press <F10>, as there's no need to provide a background text description of the field, and key in this description:

```
COURSE TITLE      TEXT       25 characters

Derivation Formula = LOOKUP "COURSE NUMBER MATCH" "COURSE TITLE"

Prevent Data-Entry = YES
```

Unlike the Lecturer Num Match relationship, this has already been described upon the database. It was one of those set inside Chapter 2 when relationships were first discussed.

Our data-entry form is now complete, so we can now press <F2> once more, this time to save the screens format upon DataEase. If you wished, you could add some instructional text and perhaps experiment with changing text colours around before saving it. But I'll leave that up to you.

In comparison to designing the data-entry screen, the DQL programming procedure is fairly straightforward. Select option 4, *Define Query*, from the DQL menu screen to begin.

The Form we are going to complete was designed during Chapter 2, and named Lecturer Course. It contains all the fields we've used upon the data-entry screen, so this makes life very easy for us. Well at least as far as the DQL code is concerned. You might be wondering why we didn't just do a simple form copy (Hot Key <F5>) to set up the data-entry screen. The reason was the need to supply a derivation formula.

Anyway, back to the DQL. Press <F9> to inform DataEase that you are going to indulge in some high-level coding. Then delete the word *For* that's in the top left-hand corner of the work area. Next press <F1> to obtain a list of all the available key words. As you are already know, the form to be recorded is named Lecturer Course. We require DataEase to enter a record by this name onto the database containing the information that's just been keyed onto the data-entry screen.

So, as you may have guessed, the command Enter a Record is the keyword to be picked from the list displayed. DataEase will next prompt for the name of the form to be used, so opt for Lecturer Course. Finally it wants to know what fields are to receive data and what information is to go into which field.

If you remember, and I'm sure you will because it was a lot of work, when data entry was first discussed in Chapter 3 your initial DQL code consisted of a long list of field names with instructions about what value was to go into each field. Subsequently, you were then told to wipe out the whole list and instead just use the phrase Copy All. I couldn't be so mean to you again, well not yet anyway, so below is listed all the DQL code that you need to write.

```
Enter a record in LECTURER COURSE
   Copy All from data-entry.
```

All very nice and straightforward. Now press <F2> to return to the DQL menu screen. Finally, as we can't test the code yet (the Lecturer Num Match relationship has still to be described remember) save the procedure naming it as Xref Lecturer\Course.

```
 _____
|                                                                                |
|  COURSE ALLOCATION                         Running procedure COURSE ALLOCATION  |
|  END OF PROCEDURE. SPACE: Return to Menu    PgUp: Scroll                        |
|                                                                                |
|                          COURSE ALLOCATION DETAILS                              |
|                                                                                |
|  ============================================================================  |
|   COURSE            COURSE               LECTURER     LECTURER                  |
|   NUMBER            TITLE                NUMBER                                 |
|  ----------------------------------------------------------------------------  |
|     001     ADVANCED ENGINEERING           0002       DR ROSEMARY BISHOP        |
|     002     BASIC COMPUTER SKILLS          0005       MR RICHARD CLANCY         |
|     003     ADVANCED SOCIAL SCIENCES       0001       DR COLIN JAMES BROWN      |
|     004     ENGLISH LITERATURE             0004       SIR JAMES LEIGHTON        |
|     005     PHYSICAL EDUCATION             0003       MR GEORGE STANTON         |
|  ============================================================================  |
|_____|
```

Lecturer Course allocation report

In order to describe the Lecturer Num Match relationship required by this procedure we need to return all the way back to the Main menu screen. So keep pressing <Esc> until that screen is reached. Once there, it is necessary to access the Form Definition menu that we first met in Chapter 2. Then select *Define Relationships* from the menu list provided.

The first relationship to be defined is the Lecturer Num Match. Using the Lecturer Number that has been keyed onto the data-entry screen we require this relationship to find a Lecturer form with a Lecturer Number field that contains the same number. So how should the Relationship definition screen be completed?

Start by identifying the Lecturer form as Form 1. Then leaving the modified field blank, move on to the Form 2 field on the screen. Problem . . . we don't wish to link the Lecturer form to another form, we need to associate it with a data-entry screen. How is that to be done? Again, the people who wrote DataEase are ahead of us. Recognising that this would be a very useful facility they made the <Esc> key a special Hot Key for just this situation.

Press <Esc> and then type in the name of the procedure, *XRef Lecturer/Course*, as the title of Form 2. DataEase will now regard the data-entry screen for that procedure as a form, allowing us to build up the rest of the relationship description in the standard manner. So, moving on down to the field boxes, we are able to record that the Lecturer Number field is to be used on both forms as the matching criteria. Finally name the relationship (for both forms) *Lecturer Num Match.*

Once that's been recorded onto the database, by pressing <F2>, *Save*, it is safe for us to return to the DQL menu screen in order to run our DQL procedure. As mentioned earlier, this procedure relies heavily upon the use of the Lecturer and Course ID codes. Therefore, we will first have to run procedures List Lecturers and List Courses – DQL code routines that will identify the required reference codes.

Now, unless you have a wonderful memory, this is going to cause a problem, as both those procedures only produce screen reports. Of course, you could get busy with a pen . . . but wouldn't it be useful if DataEase could somehow produce those reports upon a printer?

Printer Output

Well DataEase can be persuaded do just that. The subject of printer output will be covered more fully in the next chapter, but let's take a sneak look at it now.

First of all load the procedure List Courses by selecting option 8, *Load Procedure,* from the menu. Then choose that procedure from the names listed down the right-hand side of the screen, either by covering it with the highlight bar or typing in its number. DataEase will then load it into memory for you, ready to be run. Don't be unnerved by the message:

`Convert this QBE (Quick Report) into a DQL procedure?`

that will appear as the code is loaded. Simply respond with a Yes. This causes DataEase to write a DQL procedure for you based on the QBE information you supplied it earlier.

You can now go ahead and press <1>, *Run Procedure*, if you must, but all that will achieve is a screen display. It's better instead to press <6>, *Define Print Style*, and have the print definition screen appear ready for you to complete.

Without going into all the bells and whistles (Chapter 6 will be doing all that) for now, just press <2> to have the word *Printer* appear within the Report Definition box. Then using <Tab> move down the screen until you reach the box named Printer Name. Once there, press <F3> for the default printer name to appear. Now you can finish by pressing <F2> to save the report definition and return to the DQL menu screen.

If you have a printer attached, you can now run the procedure by pressing <1>, *Run Procedure*, and a list of the courses and their relevant course numbers will be produced by your printer.

Next, load the List Lecturers procedure, and following the same steps as you've just done above, obtain a print report detailing the lecturers' details. If you haven't got a printer there's no need to become concerned because all the information required is detailed below anyway. You are now ready to run the DQL routine – XRef Lecturer/Courses.

Load up the procedure and start it running. Once the data-entry screen has been displayed DataEase will patiently wait for you to enter a lecturer's number. Respond by keying in the number 1 and then press <Enter>. If everything has gone as it should DataEase will quickly reply by producing the name Dr Colin James Brown upon the screen.

Once you pressed <Enter>, it will have looked at the field definitions held on the data-entry screen for the fields Title, Christian Name and Surname, realising that they had Lookup commands that referred to a relationship named Lecturer Num Match. DataEase will then have located that relationship's description and found that it was required to find a Lecturer form that had a Lecturer Number field with a value of 1 – i.e a Lecturer form that matched the value keyed into the Lecturer Number field upon the screen. Once that had been achieved, the information held in that form's Title, Christian Name and Surname forms were to be copied onto the screen.

During Chapter 3 it was revealed that Dr Brown is a Doctor of Philosophy, and accordingly the course he is responsible for at the college is Advanced Social Sciences. This course has the number 3 as its ID code so enter that figure into the Course Number field. DataEase will once more spring into action, this time carrying out the search criteria defined by the Course Num Match relationship, in order to display the course title upon the screen. Press <F2> and that information will be recorded upon the Lecturer Course form that is to be held upon the database.

Now continue to record this course information against each Lecturer:

Lecturer No	Lecturer	Course No	Title
2	Dr Rosemary Bishop	1	Advanced Engineering
3	Mr George Stanton	5	Physical Education
4	Sir James Leighton	4	English Literature
5	Mr Richard Clancy	2	Basic Computer Skills

A similar procedure now has to be followed in order to link the students to their courses.

Student Course Allocation

As you have just seen, two elements needed to be in place in order for DataEase to record information automatically: a data-entry screen and some DQL code. Therefore let's discuss the screen that needs to be designed in order to allow our Dean to record which courses a student has elected to take.

Some method of identifying the student and courses will be required. We could request the user to type in this information in full, but, as already mentioned, this runs the risk of data being miskeyed. It's much safer to use their appropriate identifier fields, namely Student Number and Course Number. It also provides another opportunity to see the Lookup command in action, as it prompts DataEase to display the student's name etc. upon the screen for us.

Is there any other information that might be required?. Well possibly the students could be unaware of the cost of a particular course. If they could be informed of this figure BEFORE the database was updated, they could change their minds about attending the course without causing us, as the database administrator, any hassle. Remember, DataEase will not update the database until <F2> has been pressed on the data-entry screen. Were <Esc> to be keyed instead, the data-entry procedure would be simply aborted.

That being the case, let us make a mental note that the cost of the requested course needs to be displayed during data entry. We can now proceed on to design the data-entry screen. Select option 2, *Start New Procedure*, from the DQL menu screen and then press <3>, *Define Data Entry Form*, to obtain the screen design form.

The screen's title is to be *Student Course Allocation*, so type that somewhere around the middle of the second screen line. Then moving down a couple of lines provide the first field name, *Student Number*. After leaving a small gap, continue by pressing <F10> to define the field's characteristics thus:

NAME   STUDENT NUMBER
TYPE   Numeric String 4 Digits
FORMATTED STRING   No
REQUIRED   Yes

Having pressed <F2> to return to the design screen, leave another gap before pressing <F10> again. We are now going to describe the fields that we wish DataEase to automatically display for us. In this case the student's title and name.

NAME   TITLE
TYPE   CHOICE MR,MRS,MS,MISS,DR,SIR and LADY
FIELD CALCULATION   LOOKUP "STUDENT LINK" TITLE
PREVENT DATA ENTRY   Yes

It is extremely important that you remember that where a Choice field is used in association with a Lookup command, that its Choice List descriptions are **identical** and **in the same order** as those provided within the Choice field to which it is linked. Failure to adhere to this rule will result in your database information becoming corrupted and useless!

```
┌─────────────────────────────────────────────────────────────────────┐
│                                                                       │
│  Form: XREF STUDENT/COURSES   R   1 C    1                            │
│                                                                       │
│                                                                       │
│               @14   <<< STUDENT COURSE ALLOCATION >>> @11             │
│                                                                       │
│          STUDENT NUMBER                                               │
│                                                                       │
│          COURSE NUMBER                                                │
│                                                                       │
│                                                                       │
│                       COST OF COURSE = £                              │
│                                                                       │
│              Enter Student's number and Course number.                │
│                                                                       │
│              Press @13<F2@11> to update database records or           │
│                                                                       │
│                       @13<ESC>@11 to exit                             │
│                                                                       │
│                                                                       │
│                                                                       │
│  F4CMDHELP ESCEXIT F2SAVE F3CUT F5COPY F6PASTE F7DELLN F8INSLN F10FIELD│
└─────────────────────────────────────────────────────────────────────┘
```

Student Course allocation data-entry screen

The next field to be described holds the student's Christian names.

NAME	CHRISTIAN NAMES
TYPE	TEXT
LENGTH	14 Characters
FIELD CALCULATION	LOOKUP "STUDENT LINK" "CHRISTIAN NAMES"
PREVENT DATA ENTRY	Yes

Note the use of quotes around both the relationship name Student Link and the name of the field from which information is to be copied, Christian Names. This is required because the names are more than one word in length. Where the name is a single word, as with Title in the previous field description, quotes are not required.

The final field upon this line is Surname.

NAME	SURNAME
TYPE	TEXT
LENGTH	2 Characters
FIELD CALCULATION	LOOKUP "STUDENT LINK" SURNAME
PREVENT DATA ENTRY	Yes

We can now move down a couple of screen lines and start designing the course information. The first field to be described upon this line is the Course Number field that is to be used to identify the course that the student wishes to attend.

NAME	COURSE NUMBER
TYPE	NUMERIC STRING
LENGTH	3 Digits
FORMATTED STRING	No
REQUIRED	YES

Now we need a field to describe that course title:

NAME	COURSE TITLE
TYPE	TEXT
LENGTH	25 Characters
FIELD CALCULATION	LOOKUP "COURSE LINK" "COURSE TITLE"
PREVENT DATA ENTRY	Yes

Then finally we require a field that is to display the cost of the requested course. This could be defined a few lines below the course information:

NAME	COURSE FEE
TYPE	NUMBER
NUMBER TYPE	FIXED POINT
DIGITS TO LEFT	4
DIGITS TO RIGHT	2
FIELD CALCULATION	LOOKUP "COURSE LINK" "COURSE FEE"
PREVENT DATA ENTRY	Yes

```
LIST STUDENT COURSES                    Running procedure LIST STUDENT COURSES
SPACEorPgDn: Continue procedure EXIT: Abort procedure PgUp: Scroll

                    STUDENT COURSE ALLOCATION REPORT

=================================================================================
   STUDENT        STUDENTS NAME              COURSE        COURSE TITLE
    NO                                        NO
---------------------------------------------------------------------------------
   0001  SMITH        ELIZABETH       MRS    002    BASIC COMPUTER SKILLS
                                             004    ENGLISH LITERATURE
   0002  PENDLEBURY   LESTER IAN      MR     003    ADVANCED SOCIAL SCIENCES
                                             004    ENGLISH LITERATURE
                                             005    PHYSICAL EDUCATION
   0003  JERMAN       ANDREW          MR     001    ADVANCED ENGINEERING
   0004  DYER         EDWARD          MR     001    ADVANCED ENGINEERING
                                             002    BASIC COMPUTER SKILLS
   0005  ROGERS       ANGELA          MISS   004    ENGLISH LITERATURE
                                             005    PHYSICAL EDUCATION
   0006  ALEXANDER    MARY            MRS    003    ADVANCED SOCIAL SCIENCES
                                             004    ENGLISH LITERATURE
   0007  JAMES        CHRIS           MR     001    ADVANCED ENGINEERING
                                             003    ADVANCED SOCIAL SCIENCES
   0008  ADAMSON      FRANK           MR     002    BASIC COMPUTER SKILLS
```

Student Course allocation report

Our data-entry screen is then complete. For user friendliness some text lines providing instructions could also be provided. I would suggest something along the lines of:

```
Enter Student's Number and Course Number

Press <F2> to update database records or <Esc> to exit
```

The relationships used during the design of this screen were set up in Chapter 2.

Now press <F2> to save that screen format information and return to the DQL menu screen. Incidentally, it might be as well to point out at this stage that DataEase will not remember your screen design until it has been associated with some DQL code. So, if you were to leave the procedure at this point, all the hard work you've just done will disappear.

As we don't want that to happen let's hasten on to write some DQL code. Select option 4, *Define Query*, from the DQL menu. Then, once the DQL coding screen makes its appearance, delete the word *For* and then provide these code instructions:

```
Enter a record in STUDENT COURSES
    Copy all from data-entry.
```

In English that translates to:

❑ Create a record upon the database using the Student Courses form

❑ Look at the data-entry screen

❑ If there is a field upon the screen that has the same title as one upon the Student Course form, copy the information contained within that screen field into a field with the same name that's upon the Student Course record created at stage 1. e.g Copy the number keyed into the Student Number field on the screen to a field named Student Number on the Student Courses record just created.

That's the DQL procedure to record a student's course complete. So, press <F2> to return to the DQL menu screen and then select option 7, *Save Procedure* naming the code *XRef Student/Courses*.

Possibly you'll be relieved to hear that is the last bit of data entry that you will be required to endure. Once the information below has been keyed, the Porterhouse database will contain all the data it requires to furnish the reports we first discussed in Chapter 2.

Press <1>, *Run Procedure*, to enter the code:

Student Number	Student Name	Course Number	Course Title	Cost
1	Mrs Elizabeth Smith	2	Basic Computer Skills	35
		4	English Literature	40
2	Mr Ian Lester Pendlebury	3	Advanced Social Sciences	40
		4	English Literature	40
		5	Physical Education	25
3	Mr Andrew Jerman	1	Advanced Engineering	50
4	Mr Edward Dyer	1	Advanced Engineering	50
		2	Basic Computer Skills	35
5	Miss Angela Rogers	4	English Literature	40
		5	Physical Education	25
6	Mrs Mary Alexander	3	Advanced Social Sciences	40
		4	English Literature	40
7	Mr Chris James	1	Advanced Engineering	50
		3	Advanced Social Sciences	40
8	Mr Frank Adamson	2	Basic Computer Skills	35
		5	Physical Education	25
9	Mrs Fiona James	4	English Literature	40

DQL Interrogations

Possibly by this stage you are beginning to think that you cannot have a DQL procedure without a data-entry screen. Not so . . . to prove the point let's have a stab at producing the first report that the Dean of Porterhouse College requested. How many students are attending the college?

As explained earlier, this is a relatively simple procedure that requires DataEase to do no more than count the number of Student forms it has recorded. Even simpler you might be thinking, just have it display the latest Student Number, after all they are allocated in order as each student registers at the college. If so, you've forgotten to consider the possibility of a student leaving. Unless you wished to make life very complicated, the student's number, although no longer used, would have remained unique and will not have been issued to any other student. In such situations the latest Student number would not reflect the actual attendance figure. So let's keep things watertight by requesting DataEase to do a bit of counting.

Start off a new procedure from the DQL menu screen and then jump straight into option 4, *Define Query*. As usual on the DQL coding screen, DataEase will be trying to prompt us by assuming our first command is to be the word *For*. On this occasion it is quite correct, so leaving that word to stand, and select the Student form from those listed at the top of the screen. A Student form exists for every student recorded as attending the college.

Reply No to DataEase's question regarding any selection criteria as we require every such form to be counted. Feeling very confident after having you accept its earlier help, DataEase now proceeds to produce the command line List Records. For now we'll humour it by letting it have its own way and select the Student Number field to be the one we want to be used. This field stands out as the one to be chosen as it is the only field upon the record that we can truly trust to be unique.

DataEase will next want to know if we wish to have that field selected inside a group or with totals. Reply No to this question as we are not interested in the fields contents, just how many there are! You will next be asked if any more fields are to be selected. Again answer No, as this one field will be sufficient to furnish the information we require.

DataEase, feeling that it's on a run and that it has us completely in its pocket, will now return to the DQL menu where it awaits our command to run the DQL code that it proudly thinks it has written for us. If you wish immediately to shatter its smug attitude that *Computers Rule OK* move straight onto the next paragraph. Otherwise encourage its growing megalomania by pressing <1>, *Run Procedure*, to be rewarded with a screen that just displays nine student numbers.

We want the total number of students attending the college, not details of their unique reference numbers. So return to the Query by pressing option <4> once again. The code below will appear upon the screen:

```
FOR STUDENT
;
LIST RECORDS
    STUDENT NUMBER .
```

Move the cursor until it is covering the full stop that's on the last line, immediately after Student Number and delete it. DataEase recognises the full stop to mean *end of command* and we've just a little bit more to add. Staying on the same line type the symbol > (obtained by pressing <Shift> and the full stop at the same time). This symbol is used throughout the computer world to mean *is greater than* in the same way as the equals sign = is used to mean *is the same as*. An arrow going the other way < is used to represent *is less than*, while the symbol combinations <= and >= mean *is less than or equal to* and *is greater than or equal to* respectively.

Next supply the figure that we wish the Student Number figure to be tested against. As we wish every record to be used this needs to be the number zero. So key that figure before leaving another space and then typing a colon : which indicates that you wish some statistical operation to be performed.

It then only remains to inform it what operation you wish it to perform. We wish it to count the number of Student forms that it finds with a Student Number that's greater than zero so the statistical command we are going to use is Count.

Your final DQL code should now look like this:

```
FOR STUDENT
  ;
LIST RECORDS
   STUDENT NUMBER > 0 : COUNT.
```

Give the procedure a run, and instead of having nine student references displayed, a somewhat scruffy looking report will inform you that DataEase has counted nine Student forms that satisfy the criteria we laid down. Don't worry about the screen display, you will be told how to tidy that up in the next chapter. For now, simply save the procedure naming it Count Students.

The Dean's eighth question: *How many lecturers does the college employ?* can be given the same treatment. Except, that this time, instead of counting the number of Student forms, we will need to calculate the total Lecturer forms instead. The resultant DQL code reads:

```
FOR LECTURER
  ;
LIST RECORDS
   LECTURER NUMBER > 0 : COUNT.
```

This procedure should now also be saved, with the name *Count Lecturers*.

The Define Command

Some of the other points raised by the Dean also call for some calculations to be conducted. Questions 6 and 7: *How were people attracted to the college?* and *What type of people are they?* require answers that show various totals, allowing users to decide for themselves the information they require.

However, the Count command cannot help us to answer these questions. It can only be used in situations where the field being counted contains a number. In order to furnish the information required by the above two questions we will need to use fields that contain characters, to be exact, the Choice field on the Student form named Contacted. Remember, this field contains a list of the ways that Porterhouse College advertises itself. Therefore it is the best field to use to determine exactly how well those methods are working.

Armed with the knowledge that it is the Student form that is to be used and that the Contacted field upon that form contains the information to be counted, we are ready to launch ourselves once more into a DQL procedure. Hold on though, if we can't use the Count command how are we going to do our calculations? Enter the Define command.

This is used to create Temporary or Global fields. Temporary fields, as their names suggest, only exist for the time it takes a DQL procedure to run. Once the DQL procedure has been completed, any values held in those fields vanish and cannot be used again, well not until that DQL code is run again. They are unique to that procedure and cannot be used by any other DQL code routine.

Global variables on the other hand can freely travel around a number of procedures. Their values are not permanent in the same way as information recorded upon a form is, but they enjoy a longer existence than their temporary cousins. We will discuss their use in more detail during a later chapter.

For now, we need to create some temporary fields using the Define command. First it is necessary to consider how we are going to use the fields. That's no problem, they are required to be used as counters, holding the total number of times that the Contacted field holds a particular value. That tells us they need to be Number type fields.

Defined fields can have the same type as the permanent fields we've described on the forms with the exception of Choice, Dollar and Yes/No. Here are the criteria to be considered when setting up a temporary or global field:

Status	Global or Temporary
Name	Can be anything but must be contained within quotation marks.
Type	Anything except Choice, Dollar and Yes/No
Length	This property can be ignored as it is optional. DataEase making an intelligent guess in situations where no answer is provided.

We've already established most of that information except for the field names. So, maintaining the practice of sensible field and form names, let's name them for their use. We require separate totals to be calculated for the five possible values of the Contacted field, namely Word of Mouth, Local Paper, Mailshot, Radio Advert and Other. So they will be our fields names.

From the DQL menu, first select option 2, *New Procedure*, and then option 4, *Define Query*. Then once upon the DQL programming screen press <F9> to inform DataEase that we are about to indulge in some fancy high-level DQL programming. The last thing to do before we get started is to remove the *For* command word from the screen.

Field definitions can appear anywhere within a procedure as long as the fields are so defined before they are used. The standard practice, however, is to define them at the head of the procedure so that's what we shall do.

```
DEFINE TEMP "field name" type length .
```

The above statement shows the structure of the Define command. Now, here's what needs to be entered upon the screen for our procedure.

```
DEFINE TEMP "WORD OF MOUTH" number .
DEFINE TEMP "LOCAL PAPER" number.
DEFINE TEMP "MAILSHOT" number.
DEFINE TEMP "RADIO ADVERT" number.
DEFINE TEMP "OTHER" number.
```

Note how each definition ends with a full stop. DataEase will get very upset if you forget to include these.

Having defined our temporary variables we now need to provide DataEase with some instructions regarding their use. We want DataEase to look at all the Student forms and then provide totals of how many students were attracted to the college via the various methods. You may have recalled that the command For is used whenever we wish a number of forms to be processed. So you already know that the next DQL procedure instruction is to read:

```
FOR STUDENT ;
```

However, unless you've been sneakily reading the program manuals, I've probably got you stumped by the next instruction. This introduces us to another new command word named Case. If you've played around with the BASIC programming language this command will already be familiar to you as it behaves in exactly the same way.

No computer programming language, be it a mainframe language such as COBOL or PASCAL, or a PC-based language such as the aforementioned BASIC would be of much use without conditional commands. Don't be put off by the word *conditional,* it simply refers to commands that control the processing routes. I'll put that into English as well.

Assume you're at the wheel of your car. You've reached a roundabout and now have to make a decision regarding which way to turn. If your journey is to work, you need to go to the left otherwise you need to head to the right. The decision processes going on in your brain are referred to in computer circles as conditional commands. This is because they require the use of the keywords If and Else.

```
IF I'm going to work
   turn left
ELSE
   turn right.
```

These keywords If and Else, plus a few others such as Case, are used by every computer language in the world so why should DataEase be any different? Case is essentially a command that condenses a series of If . . . Else statements. You could complicate your roundabout deliberations by adding a few more conditions.

To get to the supermarket I need to go straight across, but to reach the motorway I need to take the third turning off. Home is towards the right. Our If statement is now getting a bit complicated and lengthy:

```
IF I'm going to work
   turn left
ELSE
      IF I'm going home
         turn right
      ELSE
            IF I'm going shopping
               go straight across
            ELSE
               take the third turning.
```

There is nothing wrong in writing your code inside this sort of structure but the Case command makes life a bit simpler for us. Using that command the above code would read:

```
CASE (destination)

VALUE WORK :
   go left .
VALUE HOME :
   go right .
VALUE SHOPPING :
   go straight across .
VALUE HOLIDAY :
   take third turning .

END
```

This code works by looking at the value that's held inside a field named Destination (note that the field's name has been held inside brackets) and then routing the processing dependent upon that value.

Yes, it's just as verbose but its meaning is much clearer. If a piece of code needs changing or won't work properly it's much easier to understand what's going on if the code is written as clearly as possible. Perhaps you're having some ideas regarding how we are going to put this command to work for us.

This is the next set of instructions that you need to type:

```
case (CONTACTED)

value WORD OF MOUTH :
   assign temp WORD OF MOUTH := temp WORD OF MOUTH + 1 .
```

Let's take each line in turn starting with *case (CONTACTED)*. Incidentally, the words in lower case can be written in upper, I've just used lower case in order to differentiate between the commands and Field names. This line instructs DataEase to look at the value of the Contacted Field upon each Student form it examines.

Next there's the instruction *value WORD OF MOUTH* which means: *if the value is Word of Mouth then do the following command.*

The last line reading:

assign temp WORD OF MOUTH := temp WORD OF MOUTH + 1 .

tells DataEase to add 1 to the current value of the temporary field named Word of Mouth. The structure of this line must be followed exactly for the code to work, especially important being the fullstop at the end of the line.

```
ASSIGN variable := value .
```

We can now continue to assign the rest of our temporary fields values dependent upon the setting of the Contacted field. The final complete DQL code listing is to read:

```
DEFINE TEMP "WORD OF MOUTH" number .
   DEFINE TEMP "LOCAL PAPER" number.
   DEFINE TEMP "MAILSHOT" number.
   DEFINE TEMP "RADIO ADVERT" number.
   DEFINE TEMP "OTHER" number.

for STUDENT ;

case (CONTACTED)

value WORD OF MOUTH :
   assign temp WORD OF MOUTH := temp WORD OF MOUTH + 1 .

value LOCAL PAPER :
   assign temp LOCAL PAPER := temp LOCAL PAPER + 1 .
```

```
value MAILSHOT :
   assign temp MAILSHOT := temp MAILSHOT + 1 .

value = RADIO ADVERT
   assign temp RADIO ADVERT := temp RADIO ADVERT + 1 .

value = OTHER
   assign temp OTHER := temp OTHER + 1 .

end  .
```

Don't forget the final *end* command.

If you were now to run this procedure you would be disappointed to just see a blank display appear. This is because the DQL commands do not include any display statements e.g. List Records. Not to worry this omission need not be fatal as you will find out in the next chapter. For now just save this procedure naming it as Contact Analysis.

Designing Output

During the previous chapters we've produced screen reports detailing information that's been stored upon the database. On more than one such screen, the data has been displayed in an less than attractive manner. This chapter's purpose is to show you ways and means by which the design and display of such reports can be much improved.

For instance, let's take the DQL procedure that we were writing at the end of Chapter 5 named Contact Analysis. At the moment, although the code runs through to the end without problem, no screen report is produced. That situation is about to be changed.

Start by hovering your finger over menu option number 5, *Define Modify Format*, from the DQL menu screen. This option was briefly touched upon during Chapter 4 so the screen it will cause to be displayed should not be too unfamiliar to you. To recap, it's the Display Format Definition screen, and it is used to inform DataEase which, of its many report formats, you wish to employ.

Display Formats

Columnar Format

This format causes each display field to held in an individual vertical column that is headed by the field's name. Should the field's name exceed the length of the field then it will be concatenated. This can lead to some very untidy looking reports. But it is a simple matter to tidy them up.

Name	Address	Age
Fred Bloggs	3 Letsbe Avenue	55
Jimmy Carter	12 White Meadows	44
Fiona Gibbons	10 Newton Place	24

Based on the number of fields to be displayed across the screen in this fashion DataEase calculates the number of character positions required. It informs you of the total by displaying the message:

Minimum line length for a columnar report is nnn

If more than 80 (max screen width) is required, DataEase will spread the columns over a number of pages. You can change the figure displayed, but then you will be required to edit the display formats manually so that the fields can be shown as required.

Field Per Line

The name of this format accurately describes how it causes the information to be displayed. It produces a report with each field's value being contained upon a separate line.

```
NAME                    Fred Bloggs
ADDRESS                 23 Letsbe Avenue
AGE                     55

NAME                    Jimmy Carter
ADDRESS                 12 White Meadows
AGE                     44

NAME                    Fiona Gibbons
ADDRESS                 10 Newton Place
AGE                     24
```

Record Entry

If you wish the screen report layout to reflect how the database form is designed, this format is the one to use. Remember how earlier we discussed taking care when designing forms and their field layouts. Well here's one of the reasons:

Form's Database description
```
NAME XXXXXXXXXXXXXXXX    AGE NN
ADDRESS XXXXXXXXXXXXXXXXXXXXXXX
```

Report layout
```
NAME Fred Bloggs         AGE 55
ADDRESS 23 Letsbe Avenue

NAME Jimmy Carter        AGE 44
ADDRESS 12 White Meadows
```

```
NAME Fiona Gibbons     AGE 24
ADDRESS 10 Newton Place
```

An important factor to bear in mind when using this format concerns the situation where a field's contents are required to be hidden. Remember the salary field discussed in Chapter 2? When this occurs DataEase simply leaves a blank gap where that field would normally appear upon the screen.For example, let's assume the Address field has not been requested in the report (or its been marked as a hidden field – see *View/Write Security* in Chapter 2). Then the report would appear thus:

```
NAME Fred Bloggs        AGE 55


NAME Jimmy Carter       AGE 44


NAME Fiona Gibbons      AGE 24
```

As this example was fairly trivial it didn't really matter but it could effect an otherwise well thought out display, so take care.

Template Format

This is one of the specialised formats used by DataEase. The actual screen template to be used needs first to have been described in Form Definition just as if it were a form, except that in this case, you'd be describing a display screen.

Once a template has been created, information (even from other databases) can be used to produce a report.

Graftalk Chart Format

The software house that wrote DataEase, also markets another product named DataEase Graftalk, a graphics program. This format allows you to import a graph or chart from Graftalk into DataEase and have it displayed upon the screen. This inter-product communication provides a powerful tool as data can be transferred from DataEase to Graftalk, translated into a graph, and then returned, ready to be displayed upon the screen.

Mailing List Format

If you were perhaps wishing to prepare mailing address labels for a mailshot or other purpose, this is the format for you. It allows you to group the information in a similar manner to *Field per line*, except that more than one report is generated upon a line. It's ideal for preparing output to pre-formatted label sheets.

When selected you are first prompted to supply the number of labels (groups) required to be available across the report, then the number of columns per label. This query could be better worded to read:

What is the size of the widest field being displayed?

as that is the answer it requires.

Continuing with our example names and addresses these are the instructions required to produce this report layout.

How many Labels across? 3

*How many columns per label? 20

*Translation: *What is the size of the widest field being displayed?* Answer – 20, The number of characters in the Address field.

Fred Bloggs	Jimmy Carter	Fiona Gibbons
23 Letsbe Avenue	12 White Meadows	10 Newton Place
55	44	24

Imagine each address to be on a sticky label and you can see this format's application.

Export Format

This format could be used in situations where information held upon a DataEase database is required to be exported out to another program, possibly another database or graphics package. No screen display is produced by this format. Instead DataEase passes all the information directly out to a disk file.

There are various file formats available:

Mail Merge

This format produces a file that would be acceptable to the word processing program named WordStar. Thus it allows you to merge your DataEase information into a document or report that you are producing using WordStar. Its display format produces one record per line i.e:

"Fred Bloggs","23 Letsbe Avenue",55

"Jimmy Carter","12 White Meadows",44

"Fiona Gibbons","10 Newton Place",24

Notice how the text fields are enclosed within quotation marks. If required you can request to have the Field Names reported as well, in which case they would appear as the first line in the report.

MultiMate

The name of this format gives a hint as to its purpose as reports produced using this output style can be merged with reports being written using MultiMate. When naming the output file (covered later in this chapter) be sure to add the extension .doc, e.g. DataEase.doc, as this is required in order for the file to be identified by MultiMate. Its file format is similar to Field Per Line except that the field's value appears upon the line below the field's name.

```
FULL NAME

Fred Bloggs

ADDRESS

23 Letsbe Avenue

AGE

55
```

If you have a look at how the report is to be formatted (you have no choice as DataEase, ever eager to impress, always shows you what it intends to do anyway) you will see at the bottom of the screen an additional instruction:

call MMERGE –q %m %e

This causes a special DataEase program named MMERGE to be run. It converts the file produced under this format into a style acceptable to MultiMate. There are some restrictions on the use of this format that should be borne in mind.

❑ Output file must have the extension .doc.

❑ The maximum number of records to be contained in any one report must not exceed 254. This means that if your DQL procedure finds more than 254 records to include in your report, those record numbered 255 and above will not be included in the output file. They will simply be lost.

❑ The maximum field width (size of a field) must not be larger than 156 characters.

❑ A single record i.e. the number of items listed within the DQL procedure, must not exceed 64.

❑ Any Field Names longer than 12 characters are liable to be truncated.

WordPerfect

This format creates files that are acceptable to WordPerfect. The information is output in one continuous line. Field and End of record conditions are indicated by special characters, @*[120A]* and @*[050A]* generating ^R and ^E respectively . Unless you're going to be fiddling around with the files these can be safely ignored.

Fred Bloggs @[120A] 23 Letsbe Avenue @[120A] 55 @[050A]

Graftalk

We've already met the Graftalk format earlier in this chapter – it produces a file that can be used by DataEase's companion business graphics program Graftalk. However, this file is intended to be used separately, outside DataEase, to create a graph or chart. In other words, it is a file that can be used again and again with Graftalk without requiring any further use of DataEase at all. The format file discussed earlier would only be available during the life of the DQL procedure.

Lotus 1-2-3

This format produces a file that can be used by either Lotus 1-2-3 or Lotus Symphony. As with the MultiMate format, filename extensions are important. Use .wks for files intended for version 1 of Lotus 1-2-3, the extension .wk1 for later versions, and .wrk if Lotus Symphony is to be used. When read by any of the Lotus programs the data is automatically arranged into the columnar format used by the spreadsheets.

These special considerations need to be kept in mind when using this facility:

❏ DataEase will not show you the format of the report. This means that you are unable to edit or change it in any way.

❏ The report file is not produced in ASCII format. In other words you must NEVER attempt to display the report upon the screen. Were you to do so, DataEase is liable to retaliate by crashing your PC, maybe causing some data loss.

❏ The DQL commands In Groups, In Groups with Group Totals and any statistical operator, cannot be used in conjunction with this format:

Variable Length ASCII

A very useful format this, as it allows you to transfer information out to almost any popular program, for example a word processor, that has not already been catered for elsewhere within DataEase, or maybe a BASIC module if you are into computer programming. It displays one record per line. If you are going to play around transferring data across to programs written by yourself there is one important point to remember. Should a record field not contain any data, DataEase will not set up a

Null value for that field upon the file, instead it acts as if that record field never existed!

For example:

```
DQL    FOR STUDENTS ;
   LIST RECORDS ;
   SURNAME ;
   AGE;
   WORK TEL NO
   CONTACTED.
```

The data record produced for a student with a work telephone number would have four fields, namely:

ADAMSON

40+

447925

MAILSHOT

but a record for student who didn't go out to work would only have three:

ALEXANDER

30+

WORD OF MOUTH

Therefore when writing your DQL be sure to set up default values for fields that run the risk of containing no information. This is where the Define Temp property can

come in useful:

```
DEFINE TEMP "TELEPHONE" Numeric string 6.

FOR STUDENT ;

   IF WORK TEL NO = BLANK THEN
      ASSIGN TEMP TELEPHONE := 000000.
   ELSE
      ASSIGN TEMP TELEPHONE := WORK TEL NO.
   END

   LIST RECORDS ;
      SURNAME ;
      AGE ;
      TEMP TELEPHONE ;
```

CONTACTED.

This way you can be sure that all your records contain the correct number of fields.

You may have noticed the use of the word *Blank* inside the test condition. You can use this word with any field (Numeric or Text) to mean *Contains no Information*. Also note that the temporary field has been included among those to be listed rather than the form field. Otherwise you'll be defeating the whole object of the code.

Fixed Length ASCII

As with the previous export format, Fixed Length ASCII provides a method of transferring data across from DataEase to another program. However, as its title suggests it furnishes the data in a fixed length format. This means that there are no special field or record end characters inserted into the file. So there is the possibility that importing programs could experience problems reading the data correctly. Accordingly it is recommended that this format only be used in circumstances where no other choice is available.

DIF – Data Interchange Format

This format was designed to be used by VisiCalc but can be used by many other pieces of software to import or export data. However, unless you are familiar with the DIF file format I would recommend that you give it a wide berth.

Custom Format

This format is provided in order to allow you complete freedom over the design of your reports output. You start with a blank screen and then it's up to you what you do with it. This does require quite a bit of work though so you are advised to make use one of the other available formats, perhaps editing its results to suit, whenever possible.

To make any worthwhile use of it you first need to have a good working knowledge of the DataEase formatting commands, so let's investigate those now. Here's a list of them and the groups they belong to.

Required	Page Level	Group Level	External
items	page	group header	call
end	header		
	footer		group trailer

Those held within the Required group, as indicated by the name, have to be included inside every report format that you design. In addition, they can only be used the once. If you attempt to make repetitive use of them DataEase will make its displeasure clear to you.

The Page Level group contains commands that can be used to force data to be displayed over more than one screen or print page. Group Level commands are only used in reports if grouping has been specified in the DQL code, and the number of times that they are used must match the number of groups specified in that code.

Finally the call formatting command (External group) is used to run automatically another program once a report has been fully completed. For an example of its use see the MultiMate export format command above.

Standard Report Layout

.header

Anything written between this command and the next formatting command will be treated as a report heading. As such it will appear at the top of every report screen/page.

.footer

Like .header, this command can only be used once in a report. It is used to specify the information that is to appear at the bottom of each page of the report. If utilised, it must appear immediately below the .header command, or if that is not being used, as the first formatting command of the report.

A useful property shared by both the .header and .footer commands is the ability to instruct DataEase when to start producing the relevant information. This is achieved by simply placing a page number after the command. DataEase will then await that page of the report before it starts adding data to the head/foot of a report. For example:

```
.header 3 .footer 5
```

would cause Header information to be placed upon every page after page 2, and Footer data after page 4.

items

Mandatory command. The area between it and the next command is known as the Items Area. Any information held within this area will be printed once for every record processed by the DQL code. Therefore it is usual to place inside this area the names of the fields that are to be displayed.

.group header and .group trailer

These commands are always paired together, and are known as the group level formatting commands. They are only used in situations where the DQL code has specified their use. They indicate the start and end points for each group data report.

Care must be taken to ensure that the number of times these format commands are used exactly matches their use within the DQL code.

Example DQL code:

```
For STUDENT ;
    List records ;
    AGE RANGE in groups ;
    CONTACTED in groups ;
    SURNAME .
```

Format commands

```
.header
        PERSONAL REPORT
.group header
    AGE RANGE
.group header
    CONTACTED
.items
    SURNAME
.group trailer
.group trailer
.end
```

The phrase in groups appears twice inside the DQL code, therefore two group headers and group trailers are required. The above instructions will result in a report that details which advertising methods were most successful for a particular student age range.

.end

Usually the last report format command. It is mandatory and specifies the end of record processing. Should any fields be placed after this command, for example a sum field, this field would contain a grand total taken from all the records generated by the report, such a total appearing upon the last page of the report.

.call

If this command is used it must appear as the last formatting instruction. It allows another program to be run automatically by DataEase once the report has been completed. Upon the additional program finishing its processing, DataEase will resume control of your computer.

This command has a number of parameters:

    .call PROGRAM /D %e %r

    PROGRAM = The name of the program to be called. This must include its full DOS path if it is not held in the same directory as DataEase.

    /D = The filename for any data produced by the called program.

%*e* = The name of a file, produced by DataEase, to be used by the called program.

%*r* = The name of the DQL procedure that's just been completed.

Example

```
.call C:\BASIC\REPORT.BAS %e %r
```

will cause DataEase to run the program named REPORT.BAS that is held in a directory called BASIC using the output file produced by the DQL procedure whose name is held in the variable %r. Note you do not need to specify any values for %e or %r.

Format Editing

Now that you've been bombarded with DataEase's report formatting facilities here's a chance to turn theory into practice. At the start of this chapter you were left with your finger poised over the number 5 key. Press it now to select option 5, *Define Format*, from the DQL menu.

DataEase will respond by displaying the Format Definition screen and enquiring what format you wish to use. Press <F1> to have all the available formats displayed and then choose option 6, *Custom Format*. You should now be looking at a completely blank screen.

This state of affairs can be immediately remedied by typing the words *Porterhouse Contact Report* upon the screen. Now we could leave that report title where it is, but I think you'll agree it would look better positioned more centrally and perhaps a line or two down from the top of the screen. In order to move it, first press <Insert>, the top leftmost of the bunch immediately above the cursor control keys. DataEase will acknowledge this instruction to go into Insert mode by displaying that word at the top of the screen. It is possible to toggle in and out of this mode simply by pressing the Insert key.

The wording *Porterhouse Contact Report* can now be manoeuvred into the required central position by pressing either the spacebar to move it to the right or <Delete> to move it to the left. The keys <F7> – *Delete a line* and <F8> *Insert a line* can then be used to move it down to the required line. Fine, our report's now got a title so what it needs next is some information.

Move the cursor down a couple of lines from the title and a few columns back over to the left. If you remember, this report is required to answer the question:

How were people attracted to the college?

by displaying how many people responded to each of the advertising methods. Accordingly, our DQL procedure set up some temporary fields to calculate this information. These now need to be included upon the report form.

```
CONTACT REPORT                        Running procedure CONTACT REPORT
END OF PROCEDURE. SPACE: Return to Menu   PgUp Home LEFT RIGHT Arrows: Scroll


            <<<  PORTERHOUSE CONTACT REPORT  >>>


                    WORD OF MOUTH    3

                    LOCAL PAPER      2

                    MAILSHOT         2

                    RADIO ADVERT     1

                    OTHER            0
```

Means of contact analysis report

The first such field was called Word of Mouth so type that name upon the screen before moving the cursor across a couple of columns. Now press <F10> to get DataEase to format the field's description, (shades of data-entry screen definition). The names of the temporary fields we defined in the DQL code should now be listed across the top of the screen, and a big box, within which we are going to describe the field, should be displayed on the right hand side.

Select the Word of Mouth field from those displayed, and watch as DataEase automatically sets up replies to all the other field description questions for us. It obtained this information from the field description we provided in the DQL procedure. However, there is one question, *Suppress spaces?*, that still needs to be considered. It asks whether trailing spaces in a field's value should be ignored. DataEase, hopefully is prompting us to answer No, because then it won't have so much work to do. But is that what we want?

Well, in this case, and in most others too, DataEase has correctly assumed our response. Were we to have answered Yes to this question we could have found our carefully defined screen being messed up. However, sometimes a report can be considerably enhanced by a positive response to this question. To understand why and when to use which answer, consider these two examples that make use of the fields named Surname, Christian Names and Title that appear upon the Student and Lecturer forms. It's the field sizes that we are really interested in, these being 12, 14 and 4 characters in length respectively.

Our first example is a report that simply lists student names. The fields are laid out across the screen thus:

SURNAME   CHRISTIAN NAMES   TITLE

Starting with the Suppress Spaces property set to No, the actual report would appear upon the screen looking like this:

Dyer   Edward   Mr
Rogers   Angela   Miss
Smith   Elizabeth   Mrs
Pendlebury   Ian   Mr

Note how the names stay in neat columns, each column being the width of the field, irrespective of the size of the data contained by the field. However, if the property Suppress Spaces was set Yes, the report would appear somewhat differently as the columns width would then be dependent upon the size of the information, producing a report that looked like this:

`Dyer Edward Mr`

`Rogers Angela Miss`

`Smith Elizabeth Mrs`

`Pendlebury Ian Mr`

Accordingly it is usual to leave this property set to its default value of No if lists are to be produced.

Now think about a situation where mailing addresses are being processed. In such cases we would want the name fields to be bunched together and not separated by gaping spaces. Therefore the Suppress Spaces property would need to be set to Yes for these types of report.

As our report is closer to a list, it's okay to accept DataEase's suggested response this time. So we can continue by pressing <F2> to save the field's definition and return to the Format Definition screen.

The other temporary fields now need to be placed upon the screen as well. So repeat the above procedure, moving down a couple of lines for each field named Local Paper, Mailshot, Radio Advert and Other. Once all the fields have been defined press <F2> once more to save the format definition. DataEase will return you to the DQL menu where we can now run the procedure to obtain the report displayed above.

Have a look at some of the other reports you've produced and experiment a little with these formatting commands to tidy up your displays. Unfortunately it is not possible to play around with screen colours as we did earlier when designing data entry screens. For some reason this facility has not been provided for report screens. I rather suspect the authors of DataEase felt most reports would be output to paper or file. How this is achieved is what we are moving on to discuss next.

Printer Output

It would be rather restrictive if the only way you could access the information held upon your DataEase database was via your computer monitor. Say for example, the data had to be circulated around a group of people. It is unlikely that they would enjoy having to huddle around your computer to see the fruits of all your labour . No, instead you need a way of transporting the information about. And there are two ways by which DataEase provides just this facility: outputting the data out to a printer or alternatively placing it upon a file that can be transported upon a floppy disk.

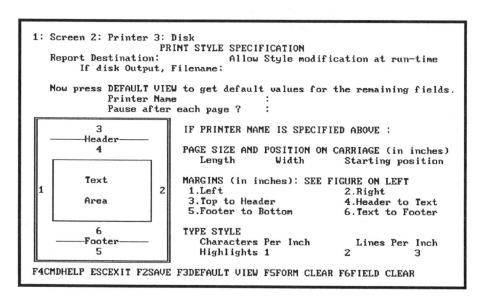

Report specification screen

One of the few options left to be discussed on the DQL menu is option number 6, *Define Print Style*. It also appears as choice number 6 on the QBE – Quick Reports menu we encountered during Chapter 4. Both these menu options operate in the same way. Select that menu option now and we'll take a look at the Print Style Specification screen. It'll probably be easier to understand if you just consider it to be another DataEase database data-entry screen that needs to be completed.

The first field requiring an answer, Report Destination, determines where the report is to be produced. You need to select from the three options provided at the top of the screen:

1 – Screen   Report displayed on screen. This is the default setting.

2 – Printer   The report is output to a printer that is attached to the computer. No screen display is produced.

3 – Disk   The report is directed to a file. This can be either upon a hard drive or a floppy disk. Again no screen output is produced.

Please opt for the Printer option at this point. Immediately you've done so the cursor will skip across the screen to the next data entry field. This prompts you to decide whether or not you will allow the decision you've just made concerning the reports destination to be overridden at run time. If you reply Yes to this question, whenever the DQL procedure is run, this Print Style Specification screen will appear, allowing each and every setting to be changed.

This facility can be very useful. Suppose a report is usually output to a printer, but occasionally you wish to check it before initiating the print report. In such a situation you'd require the output to be to screen rather than printer. What needs to be done here is initially to set up the report as a printer destination, but allow it to be amended at run time to a screen destination instead. It is not possible to request a report to go to both printer and screen, or indeed any other combination of the destination options, at the same time. Accordingly, having viewed the data it would then be necessary to re-run the procedure, this time leaving the default settings to stand in order to obtain a print output.

The default setting for this field is No, so leaving that as it is, move down to the next field. Were we to be producing a disk output this field would be used to provide the file name for the report. Incidentally, if a report was usually set up to produce printer output but was occasionally sent to a disk instead, as the printer commands are already in place, DataEase would produce the disk file complete with printer control characters. This is because it assumes that the file will later be passed to another printer, rather than be processed by a computer program. If this is not the case then be sure to make the printer fields blank when adjusting this screen at run time.

Our print style specification could be considered to be complete at this point were we to producing a disk or screen file. All that would be required would be to press <F2> to save our definition to file. However, as we are planning a print report we need to supply DataEase with some more information: the name of our printer.

Now, if you are like me, your printer gets called lots of interesting names, particularly when it decides to chew up the paper rather than print on it. Alas DataEase is not interested in these types of names, rather in the type and make you are going to be using.

Life can be very easy at this point or rather difficult. Let's take the simple path first and assume you've got a printer defined on the System Configuration Form. In this case all that is required at this point is to press <F3> and watch DataEase supply all the rest of the answers. Once it's finished showing off how clever it can be, press <F2>, *Save*, as our output definition is complete. The DQL procedure can now be run, causing your printer to spring into life, assuming you've got it switched on, of course!

Life being what it is, however, I suspect that no such printer has been defined, in which case there is a little more work to do before we can persuade DataEase to chat nicely to your printer. Hit <Esc> (gently) to take you back to the DQL menu screen and save your procedure using option 7. Then play with <Esc> again until you arrive back on the very first DataEase menu screen, the one with seven options on it starting with Form Definition and Relationships.

Once there, select option 7, *System Administration*, to access the Administration menu screen. This screen allows you, as the Database manager, to customise your system configuration and generally administer the DataEase environment. While that all sounds very grand, at this moment we are only interested in setting up our default printer. But we will encounter this menu again in later chapters.

```
Printers
Record 59 on screen
                   P R I N T E R   D E F I N I T I O N          Pg 1 of 2

         Name                    Epson FX-80
         Default Paper Width      8.5    inches (normally 8.5)
         Line Advance String     0D0A           (normally 0D0A)
         Form Advance String     0C             (normally 0C)
         Initialization String                  (start of report)
         Termination String      0C             (end of report)

      CHARACTERS PER INCH            LINES PER INCH              SET PAPER LENGTH
      CPI    Turn-on String      LPI    Turn-on String      Inches  Turn-on String
  1: 10    * 1B50            1: 6    * 1B'2            1: 11    * 1B43000B
  2: 12      1B'M            2: 8      1B'0            2: 8.5     1B4300'8
  3: 17.16   0F             3: 10.28  1B'1            3: 14      1B43000E
  4: 5       1b'W01         4:                        4:
                                                      ( * indicates default value )

                     SPECIAL EFFECTS    (Define all applicable)
      EFFECT         TURN-ON STRING              TURN-OFF STRING
      Boldface    1B'E                        1B'F
      Underline   1B2D01                      1B2D00
      Italicize   1B'4                        1B'5
F4CMDHELP ESCEXIT F2SAVE Sh-F1TABLE F3VIEW F7DEL F8MODIFY F9QBE F10MULTI
```

Printer definition screen

DataEase already has a lot of information stored away about printers. If you select menu option 3, *Define Printers*, and then go into Table View Mode (press <Shift>and <F1>) you will obtain a list of all the printers that DataEase recognises. It runs over a number of screens, so play with <PgUp> and <PgDn> while you search for the name of your particular printer. Hopefully you'll find it listed here. If not you will have to describe it to DataEase upon this form by making judicious use of your printer handbook. This is a thankless and time consuming task so I hope it is not one you have to undertake.

Having checked that your printer is known to DataEase now return to the Administration menu and select option number 2, *Define Configuration.* The form presented here describes to DataEase your database system set up, the video display in use, the printer ports, and directory information about where to find database files. The first field holds video information so leave that to stand – *Blank = VGA* colour capabilities. Move down instead to the first field that's held inside a box headed *Port Type.*

If you have a look around the back of your computer you will see a lot of wires sticking out. One of these will be attached to your printer. Now trace it back to the hole by which it enters your computer. This hole is called a port, why I don't know, but there it is. Every such hole, sorry port, upon your computer has a name and description. These make a great deal of sense to computer people but alas not much to anyone else. However, it is important that you provide DataEase with the correct information (names) otherwise it will send your printer to the computer equivalent of Coventry, refusing even to acknowledge its existence.

Printer wires generally come in two flavours: Serial and Parallel. Serial wires, being a single wire, carry data one chunk at a time. Parallel wires on the other hand consist of eight separate pieces of wire in a row, thus they are able to carry eight pieces of information at a time. Accordingly they are much faster at transporting information than serial wires. All this doesn't matter a hoot to your printer, which unless it has all sorts of Go-Faster striped accessories attached to it, can only handle one piece of information at a time anyway. Still, that's the computer industry for you!

What's important about all this is that it is fairly simple to tell a serial port from a parallel port by the size of the plug thing that goes into it. If it's fairly broad its a pretty safe bet that it's a parallel port, A slimmer port, like the one leading to your monitor, would be a serial port.

So have a look at your printer port, determine its likely description (parallel or serial) and then type that into this field. Don't worry about getting it wrong and damaging your computer or database. If you guess wrongly, the worse that will happen is that you won't get any prints.

DataEase next wants to know which number port you are using to communicate with your printer. This is usually number 1, so enter that number. If it doesn't work then change it to 2, but you should be fairly safe with 1. Finally we have to tell it the name of your printer, and this will be whichever name you found in the Printer Definition Table.

```
Configuration
1: Color 2: Monochrome 3: Color card - Mono screen
                                                        Pg 1 of 5
                      SYSTEM CONFIGURATION

    SCREEN STYLE                    (Leave blank for system default)

    PRINTERS          PORT TYPE   PORT NUMBER   PRINTER DEFINITION
          Local 1 :   parallel    1             Epson MX-80
          Local 2 :
          Network 1 :
          Network 2 :

    Default Printer : Local 1

    If a printer with SERIAL PORT is used, specify the following:

    Baud rate :        Parity :       Stop Bits :        Word length :
    Protocol  :


    DIRECTORY FOR TEMPORARY FILES
          (Leave blank to create temporary files in data directory)
```

System configuration screen

If your port was parallel then simply press <F2> at this point because enough information has been passed to DataEase for it to communicate with your printer. Return to the DQL menu, load up your procedure, access the Print Style Specification screen and describe your printer using the <F3> key.

Those of you with serial printer ports have a little more work to do I'm afraid. At the bottom of this screen DataEase is asking for information about such things as Baud rate, Parity, Protocol, etc. I can do little to help you here as your responses will depend on the type of printer you are using. But you should be able easily to determine this information from your printer manual.

Baud rate   The speed at which data is transferred along your bit of wire. DataEase can accept these values: 110,150,300,600,1200,2400,4800 and 9600 bits per second.

Parity   This is used to check that data is being received correctly by the printer. Can be set to Even, Odd or None.

Stop Bits   Defines the size of the units used to check the status of a transmission. Possible values are 1 or 2.

Word Length   How long are the message units – 7 or 8 bits?

Protocol   Strange question this one, as DataEase only accepts one protocol XON/XOFF to specify the printer's stop/start protocol. So why does it ask? Still, you now know the answer.

7

Transaction Processing

Hopefully by this stage in the Guide you are feeling more confident about writing your own DQL procedures. To date we have concentrated on procedures that only involve a single form. It is now time to start considering more complicated DQL code that will allow us to link one form's information with that of another.

An immediate case in point involves the processing required to calculate a student's course costs and fees. If you remember when we registered our students with the college we also recorded their enrolment fee. However, although they were later informed of the cost of each course, no calculation has taken place to record their full liability towards the college. Accordingly we are now requested by the Dean to perform this task.

So let's plan together what exactly it is that we require our DQL procedure to do. First, we need to decide what information we want and then identify which forms hold that data. It's a good idea to write out a list at this time, just so that nothing gets forgotten.

Information Required	Form	Field
Student's Name	Student	Surname
		Title
		Christian Names
Title of Courses	Student Courses	Course Title being attended
Cost of Course	Course	Course Fee

Now that we've identified the information and those forms upon which it is recorded, we need to think of a way of linking those forms together in a chain. In other words what relationships exist between the forms? In Chapter 2 I explained that relationships come in two types:

❑ *Ad Hoc:* The relationship only exists for the life of a DQL procedure and is unique to that procedure

❑ *Predefined:* Has an unlimited life span and can be used by many procedures.

Two predefined relationships were set up in Chapter 2 that could be used here, namely Costing and Student Number Match. But we are only going to use one of them in the DQL code we are going to write, in order that the use of both types of relationships can be demonstrated.

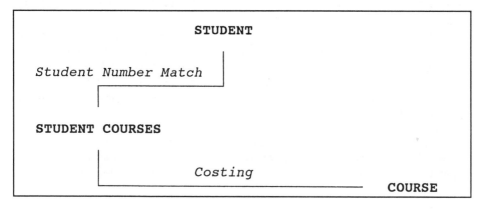

Linking the forms using predefined relationships

The diagram shows how we could link the three forms using those predefined relationships. Of these Student Number Match is the one that is going to be replaced with an Ad Hoc relationship in the DQL code. The Student Number field will still be used as the key field however.

```
COLLEGE FEES                             Running procedure COLLEGE FEES
SPACEorPgDn: Continue procedure EXIT: Abort procedure PgUp: Scroll

                PORTERHOUSE COLLEGE STUDENT COURSE FEES
-----------------------------------------------------------------------

   MR FRANK ADAMSON

                COURSE TITLE                    COST
                ------------------------        --------
                BASIC COMPUTER SKILLS           35.00
                PHYSICAL EDUCATION              25.00
                                                --------
                        TOTAL COURSE FEES       60.00
   MRS MARY ALEXANDER

                COURSE TITLE                    COST
                ------------------------        --------
                ADVANCED SOCIAL SCIENCES        40.00
                ENGLISH LITERATURE              40.00
                                                --------
                        TOTAL COURSE FEES       80.00
```

Output from the College Fees DQL procedure

Navigate through the menus until you are sitting on the DQL menu. Then select option 2, *Start New Procedure*, before using option 4, *Define Query*. There's no need to construct a data-entry form for this procedure as we are going to be processing all the student forms and thus there is no requirement to identify a particular student.

Once upon the Procedure Definition screen we'll find that DataEase has already supplied the first key command of the DQL code for us, namely the word *For*. However, if you glance at the bottom of the screen you'll see that it has also put us into Low level mode. In order to use the multiple For commands required by our procedure (we are going to identify the need for DataEase to handle more than one form) we must be in High level mode. DataEase only allowing one For command at the lower level. We can quickly adjust the level setting by pressing <F9> to toggle between mode settings.

The major form, has already been identified as Student, because every one of those forms will need to be accessed before we can identify which of the other forms are required. Therefore our first command needs to tell DataEase to read every Student Form.

`For STUDENT ;`

Our navigation diagram shows that the next form to be accessed is named Student Courses. We want DataEase to process every Student Courses form that is associated with the Student form it has just read. This way we can identify which courses a particular student is taking. Once again the For command is brought into play, our second line of DQL reads:

`for STUDENT COURSES`

As it stands that command will just instruct DataEase to read every Student Courses record it can find, regardless of the student's identity. The code needs to be tightened so that only those belonging to the student identified by the Student form are accessed. Enter our Ad Hoc relationship code on line 3:

The structure of this line follows this format:

`with (CURRENT FORM FIELD = MATCH FORM MATCH FORM FIELD)`

where:

with   Specifies the criteria for selecting a record

Current Form Field The name of the field upon the current form whose value is to be used in the match.

Match Form   The name of the form to be matched with the current form

Match Form Field The name of the field upon the Match Form whose contents are to be matched against those of the Current Form Field.

What are we going to identify as our Current Form Field, Match Form and Match Form Field?. The current form at this stage in the code is Student Courses, the Student Number field upon that form we've already said will be our key field, so that will act as our Current Form Field.

What form is the Student Courses form to be linked to? Yes, the Student form, so that becomes the Match Form. Finally what field upon the Student form are we to use as a key field? Well, Student Number is the obvious candidate. So that's our Match Form Field identified, so now we can add a third line to the code:

```
with (Student Number = STUDENT Student Number)
```

It appears that we still have one more link to make in our form chain, that between the Student Courses form and the Course fee. But as a predefined relationship named Costing already describes that link, the work has already been done for us. Accordingly the next line of our code can instruct DataEase to start a report, namely:

```
list records
```

All that remains now to do is to tell DataEase what fields to include in that report:

```
SURNAME in groups with group totals ;
```

The above command informs DataEase that we wish the report to be in Group format, each group containing information pertaining to the Surname taken off the Student form and to maintain separate totals for each such grouping. In plain English – DataEase is to separate its report up into groups, each only containing information about one student. If any calculations are performed, a separate total must be maintained for each group.

The next couple of lines are fairly standard:

```
TITLE ;
   CHRISTIAN NAMES ;
```

and then we need to start making use of the Costing relationship. Here the format of the instruction follows these rules:

```
all RELATIONSHIP RELATIONSHIP FIELD NAME
```

all	Causes every record that satisfies the relationship criteria to be processed
Relationship	The name of the predefined relationship
Relationship Field Name	The name of the field upon the linked form that is to be used.

The relationship is named Costing, and the fields that are to be used from the Course form, linked by that relationship, are Course Title, (as the Course form at this stage of the code is the Prime form we might as well take it from there as from the Student Courses form) and Course Fee. Therefore the next two lines of code could look like this:

```
all COSTING COURSE TITLE ;
   all COSTING COURSE FEE.
```

But we want to enhance the report a little by having the courses listed in alphabetical order. So the first line needs a slight addition:

```
all COSTING COURSE TITLE in order ;
   all COSTING COURSE FEE ;
```

Note that the original full stop after Fee has been replaced by a semi-colon. The reason? Well it would be nice if we could persuade DataEase to add up all a students' course fees to provide us with a total liability figure for each student. This can be achieved by the addition of one more line:

```
all COSTING COURSE FEE : sum .
```

Finally each For command must have a matching End instruction to mark the end of each For's processing commands. We have two Fors, therefore to complete our DQL code we must furnish two Ends. Should you ever fail to match up your Fors and Ends you can be sure that DataEase will take every opportunity to complain about it!

The complete DQL code should read:

```
for STUDENT ;
   for STUDENT COURSES
      with (Student Number = STUDENT Student Number)
         list records
            SURNAME in groups with group totals ;
            TITLE ;
            CHRISTIAN NAMES ;
            all COSTING COURSE TITLE in order ;
            all COSTING COURSE FEE ;
            all COSTING COURSE FEE : sum .
   end
end
```

It's not the most elegant piece of code but it gets the job done. Doubtless, as you get more expert and experienced at playing with DataEase, and DQL in particular, you'll find ways of improving upon it. Speaking of practice, when you run the above code the screen display is unlikely to match the one shown at the head of this chapter. You will need to play with the report formatting commands detailed in Chapter 6 if you wish it to do so. Once you've written this code it should be saved as College Fees.

Hopefully you can now see how information contained upon a number of forms can be linked to produce a single report.

Amending Records

Now following on from that procedure, and having taken a look at the Student form, it is apparent that there is some data missing off that form, namely the information to be recorded in the fields named Course Fees and Total Charged. Having run the above code we now have the accounting information available, so why don't we just use option 2, *Record Entry*, on the main menu to update those records. Well we could, but it would be a bit like having a dog and barking yourself. It would be a much better idea to get DataEase to do it for you, and it won't make any silly accounting errors.

We have already identified which forms and fields are required. So we can go straight on in, and start determining the boundaries of the DQL procedure we are going to write to do this job.

Every Student form is to be updated with accounting information. This data is to be calculated by totalling the fees required for courses undertaken by the student, such data being held on the Course forms which can be accessed via the Student Courses form. To do this we will need to maintain a running record of the course fees, so a temporary field will also be required.

Here is the code, named Student Liability, for you to look at and copy. Ignore the line numbers, they are just there to provide reference points for when the code's logic is explained.

```
1    define temp "RUNNING TOTAL" number .

2    for STUDENT ;
3       assign temp RUNNING TOTAL := 0 .


4       for STUDENT COURSES
              with (Student Number = STUDENT Student Number)


5          for COURSE
                  with (COURSE NUMBER = STUDENT COURSES COURSE NUMBER)
6             assign temp RUNNING TOTAL := temp RUNNING TOTAL +
                                                        COURSE FEE .
7          end


8       end

9    modify records
10       COURSE FEES    := temp RUNNING TOTAL ;
11       TOTAL CHARGED := temp RUNNING TOTAL + ENROLMENT FEE .
12   end
```

You may have noticed that all the relationships are Ad Hoc. Our hand was forced in this direction by the need to update the temp field Running Total from a field upon the Course form. DataEase will not accept Relationship names inside formulae used to update temporary fields. Hence we had to point directly to the Course form by making it the Current form, i.e. the form last pointed to by a For command.

Let's quickly run through the logic of the code, line by line.

1 – A temporary variable is declared to act as a running total field.

2 – DataEase is instructed to read every Student form that it has recorded upon the database.

3 – Set the temporary variable to zero. If it was not reset as each new Student record is accessed then an accumulative total would result for ALL the students rather than each individual as is required

4 – DataEase is next instructed to process all the Student Courses forms that have the same Student Number as that held upon the Student form. These are required in order to allow us to link through to the Course forms, there being no possible direct means of establishing such a link.

5 – Then it is told to read all the Course forms holding the same value in their Course Number fields as that held in a field of that name upon the Student Courses form.

6 – Having obtained a Course form that satisfies those conditions DataEase is now told to add the Course Fee onto the Running Total value.

7 – It is to keep doing so until it can find no more Course forms to process.

8 – Forces DataEase to go back to line 4 in order to read in another Student Courses form. Lines 4, 5, 6, 7 and 8 will continue to go around in a loop until no more Student Courses forms are available.

9 – Having processed all the students course information and calculated the course fees due, DataEase is now told to modify (Update/Amend) the Student record. The two preceding End statements re-establish that form as the current form. See how important it is to place your End statements in the correct positions inside your code.

10 – The field Course Fees upon the Student form is set to the value of the Running Total field.

11 – The Total Charged field upon that record is updated by a figure calculated by adding the Running Total field to the value of the Enrolment Fee field.

12 – The final End statement causes DataEase to repeat steps 1 through to 12 again and again, until all the student records have been processed.

Control Procedures

All the DQL procedures that we have covered to date are collectively known as *Processing* procedures. Such procedures allowing you to create, modify, delete and list records, plus of course design the report outputs, i.e. screen or print reports. There is, however, another type of procedure that DataEase will recognise. This is called a *Control* procedure.

Basically, Control procedures provide a method of linking Processing procedures, such that they can be run automatically, one behind the other. The final piece of DQL code we are going to write together makes use of a Control procedure to link four of the Processing procedures we've already written, albeit with a few slight modifications to their code. As a result we will be able to record a new student's name and address details, the courses they wish to attend, and then produce a printed bill that displays all the relevant course information and the amount they are required to pay to the college. All by running one single Control procedure.

Control procedures do have some limitations, however, as they themselves cannot do any of the record creation, updating, etc. – tasks that Processing procedures can carry out. But they can link as many procedures (Control or Processing) as you wish, in order to achieve whatever it is you require them to do. They can also directly invoke many of the operations that have previously only been available via the DataEase menu system, for example Record Entry and Reorganize.

Here is a table of the 35 DQL commands that can be used within DataEase. They fall into three groups:

❑ *Control:* Commands that can only be used by Control procedures

❑ *Processing:* Commands suitable only for Processing procedures

❑ *Any Procedure:* Commands that can be used by either type.

Don't worry over much about storing them away inside your own memory database as DataEase will be only too eager to point out any errors you might make.

Command Number	Command	Group
1	List Records	Processing
2	Modify Records	Processing
3	Delete Records	Processing
4	Enter a Record	Processing
5	For	Processing
6	Lock	Processing
7	Unlock	Processing
8	Query Selection	Processing
9	Input	Processing
10	Output	Any Procedure

11	Message	Any Procedure
12	If	Any Procedure
13	Else	Any Procedure
14	End	Any Procedure
15	While	Any Procedure
16	Break	Any Procedure
17	Exit	Any Procedure
18	Case	Any Procedure
19	Value	Any Procedure
20	Others	Any Procedure
21	Define	Any Procedure
22	Assign	Any Procedure
23	.	Any Procedure
24	Run Procedure	Control
25	Call Menu	Control
26	Call Program	Control
27	Record Entry	Control
28	Import	Control
29	Reorganize	Control
30	DB Status	Control
31	Backup DB	Control
32	Restore DB	Control
33	Lock DB	Control
34	Unlock DB	Control
35	Install Application	Control

```
COLLEGE FEES                          Running procedure COLLEGE FEES
END OF PROCEDURE. SPACE: Return to Menu    PgUp: Scroll

                   PORTERHOUSE COLLEGE REGISTRATION CHARGES

    STUDENT   MRS KAY LEWIS

                    COURSE TITLE                        CHARGE
             ------------------------------          -----------
             ADVANCED SOCIAL SCIENCES                    40.00
             ENGLISH LITERATURE                          40.00


                                                     -----------
             TOTAL COURSE FEES                           80.00
             ENROLLMENT FEE                              25.00
                                                     -----------
             TOTAL DUE                                  105.00
```

Detailed student registration bill

Time for some hands-on experience of writing Control procedures. As detailed above our final piece, or rather pieces, of DQL code are going to considerably automate the procedure of registering and billing a new student. As always we need to start by thinking about what we want the procedure to do. Once more a list becomes useful:

Procedures Required	Title	Status
To record a student's name and address	Record New Student	Written
To record the courses to be taken	Registration	Required
To calculate cost of courses and update Student record	Student Liability	Written
To print student's college bill	College Fee	Written
To run these procedures automatically	Registration TP	Required

Although some of the procedures have been given a status of *written*, this is not completely true. It would perhaps be better to say that they require some minor amendment. However, it does let us differentiate between them and the code that's still to be designed and written.

I'm going to start by detailing the Control procedure code. The subsequent amendments to the existing code will then hopefully make more sense, than if we tackled them straight from the start. For all its grand title, writing a Control procedure is a very straightforward business, far simpler than a Processing procedure in fact. Here's the code required for our the Registration TP Control procedure. You write it upon exactly the same screen as Processing procedures, i.e option 4, *Define Query*, from the DQL menu screen.

```
define global "STUDENT ID" Numeric String 4 .
define global "RUN STATUS" Text 8 .
run procedure "RECORD NEW STUDENT" .
if global RUN STATUS = "CONTINUE" then
    run procedure "REGISTRATION" .
    run procedure "STUDENT LIABILITY" .
    run procedure "COLLEGE FEES" .
end
```

We've met the Define command before, but this is the first time its been used with the Global attribute. It is no different to the Temp attribute save that the value held by the field is made available to a number of DQL procedures, rather than remaining the sole property of one. To pass a value between procedures it is necessary to have the global field declared in each and every procedure. In this Control procedure two such variables are declared. Field Student ID is to carry the value of the unique Student Number that will be allocated to a new student by the procedure Record New Student. It will then be available to all the ensuing procedures, while Run Status is used as a *flag* variable to denote the current status of the processing.

Flag variables are not unique to DataEase. In fact it's true to say that almost every computer program in existence makes some use of them. They are nothing special, they simply act as carriers of condition values. Someone writing a shoot-'em-up computer game would use flags to decide if an alien had been hit. The flag variable, perhaps named *dead alien*, would initially be set to No and then once the creature from Athos II had been spliced in two by an expertly aimed laser beam, the value of *dead alien* would be changed to Yes. The computer program, by checking out the value of the flag field, can then decide what actions to take, either to crown you Emperor of the Universe or relegate you to cleaning the outside of spaceships.

In our procedure it is used to indicate whether or not <Esc> (the Hot Key that abandons processing) was pressed during the run of the Record New Student procedure. If it was (Run Status = Blank), there would be no requirement for the other procedures to be run, hence their appearance inside the conditional statement. If it wasn't (Run Status = Continue), all those procedures would be run, one after the other in the sequence they are listed. The way that the global variable Run Status gets assigned either of these two values will be covered in a moment.

The next new command inside this procedure is Run Procedure. It means exactly what is says: *Go and run this procedure.* The order in which such statements appear govern the sequence in which each procedure is called.

Therefore. in English, our code is saying:

1 – Set up a couple of global variables named Student ID and Run Status.

2 – Run the procedure named Record New Student.

3 – Check the value of the global variable named Run Status.

4 – If it has a value of Continue then:
    a – Run the procedure named Registration
    b – Then run the procedure named Student Liability
    c – Finally run the procedure named College Fees.

And that basically is all there is to a Control procedure. So write that code, save it as TP Processing and then we can move on to discuss the Processing procedures.

Now that you have some idea how the Control procedure wishes to make use of them you'll have a better understanding of the tinkering that we are going to do with them.

First – Record New Student. This procedure was left to you to write at the end of Chapter 3. If you cheated and skipped that exercise, please return to that chapter and do it now, because otherwise our Control procedure just isn't going to work. Mind you I suspect you already know that, as a few of the other DQL procedures would have lacked that final something if you neglected to play the game earlier on.

The code at the moment consists of a fairly complicated and busy data-entry screen and a few lines of DQL code that read:

```
Enter a record in STUDENT

Copy all from data-entry ;

DATE ENROLLED := current date .
```

Well you'll no doubt be pleased to hear that the data-entry screen requires no changes at all. It can be left to stand. Not so, however, the code. It requires a few enhancements before it can be allowed to play with the Control procedure. The first change involves declaring the Global variables. Remember that these must be declared inside each individual procedure that makes use of them, as well as within the Control procedure itself. So add those lines to the beginning of the code:

```
Define global "STUDENT ID" Numeric String 4 .
Define Global "RUN STATUS" Text 8.

Enter a record in STUDENT
   etc , etc
```

Fine, now our two procedures can pass field values inbetween each other. But what values are to be sent? The responsibility for setting up these fields contents lies with the Record New Student procedure. So let's think about how that is to be achieved.

The global variable Student ID needs to be set to the value of the Student Number Field held by the Student record created by this procedure. We could try putting a line reading:

```
assign global STUDENT ID := STUDENT Student Number .
```

inside the Enter a Record code routine. But we can't do that for two reasons: one DataEase won't let us write it there, and two it wouldn't work if it did, because the record hasn't been created yet!

The way around this problem is to place the statement on its own and make it point to the specific Student record that we are interested in. So, add this code to the end of the DQL statements:

```
assign global STUDENT ID := any STUDENT with
   ( SURNAME = data-entry SURNAME and
   CHRISTIAN NAMES = data-entry CHRISTIAN NAMES
            and TITLE = data-entry TITLE )
   Student Number .
```

This code tells DataEase to find a Student record that has the same surname, christian names and title details as were entered upon the data-entry screen. And then set the global field Student ID to the value of the Student Number field upon that record.

The value placed inside the Student ID field is now available to all the other procedures, providing, of course, they have it declared as a global variable. Now for the field we are using as a flag, namely Run Status.

When I was explaining the use of flag fields earlier, and how in particular this field was going to be used, I made reference to two values. One value, Blank, would signal to the control procedure that <Esc> had been pressed, causing it to return control to DataEase after this procedure. The alternative setting of Continue would allow the other DQL procedures to be run. Logically, therefore, somewhere inside this procedure, we must allocate first one and then the other of these values to this field. But whereabouts and in which order?

That's not quite the case, however, because the value of the field automatically defaults to Blank so that's one problem out of the way. But what about assigning a value of Continue?

Well, what do we want it to denote? This global field is being used as a flag to signal whether or not <Esc> had been pressed. Think about when it is possible to use that button. Will it be while the data-entry screen is being displayed or while the Student record is being created upon the database. By the time DataEase is happily making a new record for us, it's too late for that key to be used. The action it cancels is already taking place!

Therefore such an event as the pressing <Esc> can only occur while the data-entry screen is available and before <F2> has been keyed. Therefore a good place to put the command would be at the end of the code. After all, in order for processing to have reached that far, a Student record would have had to have been placed upon the database. Accordingly that's where it is to be written. The final code should read:

```
define global "STUDENT ID" Numeric String 4 .
   define global "RUN STATUS" Text 8 .

enter a record in STUDENT
   copy all from data-entry ;
   DATE ENROLLED := current date .

assign global STUDENT ID := any STUDENT with ( SURNAME = data-entry
SURNAME and CHRISTIAN NAMES = data-entry CHRISTIAN NAMES and TITLE =
data-entry TITLE ) Student Number .

assign global RUN STATUS := "CONTINUE" .
```

The DQL code can now be saved back onto file as Record New Student. We next have to consider the new procedure that has to be written – Registration.

```
 REGISTRATION                              Running procedure REGISTRATION


              << PORTERHOUSE COLLEGE CURRICULUM >>
        NO          COURSE TITLE              COST

        001  ADVANCED ENGINEERING            50.00

        002  BASIC COMPUTER SKILLS           35.00

        003  ADVANCED SOCIAL SCIENCES        40.00

        004  ENGLISH LITERATURE              40.00

        005  PHYSICAL EDUCATION              25.00

             COURSE  1    2    3    4    5

        Select the required course by setting to 'Y'

        Press <F2> to update database or <ESC> to exit

 F4CMDHELP ESCEXIT F2SAVE F5FORM CLEAR F6FIELD CLR
```

The Registration data-entry screen

Its purpose is to record the courses that our new student is going to take. Earlier we wrote a procedure named XRef Student Courses (Chapter 5) which captured this information for us. Could it be used here? The honest answer is yes, well perhaps with just a few minor changes such as declaring the global variables. But I want you to consider the question of user friendliness for a moment. Were a student to be taking all five of the courses available at Porterhouse College the data-entry screen associated with that procedure would need to be completed five times. Plus the student and course numbers would have to be rekeyed upon every occasion. I don't think such a strategy would be too popular with any users of your database. Writing a new procedure provides an opportunity to solve that problem.

We already know the student's unique identity code, Student Number , as that is being passed around inside the global variable Student ID. So we don't need to keep having that information resupplied. That leaves the course codes. Again in order to key these into the data-entry screen provided by the XRef Student procedure they would need to be on hand, perhaps on a piece of paper.

It would be much easier, and more professional, to present this sort of information at the time data is being keyed. Hence the data-entry screen that's just been shown. It provides the names and costs of each of the five courses and allows the students to register all their required courses upon a single screen. All that is needed now is the procedure that controls the display and processing of that screen and its information. Enter *Registration*.

Now before we get started writing this DQL code I must warn you that this procedure has elements of *hard coding*. Thus, while it's robust enough for the needs of this book where only five courses are available, it's use would not be practical where greater numbers of elements are being used. Hard coding is a computerspeak term for a piece of code where actual values are used in the place of field names. The line of code below is an example. The variable Run Status can never have any other value than Completed.

```
assign global RUN STATUS := "COMPLETED"
```

However, were the code to read thus:

```
assign global RUN STATUS := STUDENT SURNAME
```

it would be set to what ever value the Surname field upon the Student form had at the time in question. In other words it can vary. Hard coded code cannot as it has rigid values.

To business . . . Our first task is the design of the data-entry screen. It involves the use of a number of relationships in order to have the course titles and their costs automatically displayed. I'll take you through the steps required to produce the first couple of lines and then leave you to produce the other course lines. All the required relationships were set up during Chapter 2.

No	Course Title	Cost
<1>	<2>	<3>
<4>	<5>	<6>

Field <1>   Name = COURSE NUMBER1
                   Type = Numeric String
                   Size = 3
                   Derivation Formula = 1
                   Prevent Data Entry = YES

Field <2>   Name = COURSE TITLE1
                   Type = Text
                   Size = 25
                   Derivation Formula = LOOKUP COURSE1 "COURSE TITLE"
                   Prevent Data Entry = YES

Field <3>   Name = FEE1
                   Type = Number
                   Digits to left of decimal = 3
                   Digits to right of decimal = 2
                   Derivation Formula = LOOKUP COURSE1 "COURSE FEE"
                   Prevent Data Entry = YES

Field <4>   Name = COURSE NUMBER2
                   Type = Numeric String
                   Size = 3
                   Derivation Formula = 2
                   Prevent Data Entry = YES

Field <5>   Name = COURSE TITLE2
                   Type = Text
                   Size = 25
                   Derivation Formula = LOOKUP COURSE2 "COURSE TITLE"
                   Prevent Data Entry = YES

Field <6>   Name = FEE2
                   Type = Number
                   Digits to left of decimal = 3
                   Digits to right of decimal = 2
                   Derivation Formula = LOOKUP COURSE2 "COURSE FEE"
                   Prevent Data Entry = YES

Perhaps you can see a pattern emerging. The field named within the No column indicates which relationship is to be used in the derivation formulae for the course title and cost fields. You may have also noticed that the relationship names go in sequence . . . Course1, Course2 etc., reflecting the number of the line within which they are used. The derivation value of the No column field also increases in value to mirror the line number. Finally it is very important to Prevent Data Entry, otherwise when your screen appears, the values you want won't!

Can you see how the display works?. The relationships are all built around the value of the No column field. Depending upon its value the associated Title and Fee fields will be set up to show that course numbers details. For example, the first field in the No column named Course Number1 has a value of 1. The Course1 relationship set up in Chapter 2, instructed DataEase to use this value to go and find a Course record with the same number. Having done so, it will then place the Course Title upon that record into the title field (Course Title1) upon the screen, and also the Course Fee value into its screen field which is named Fee1. Then it will do the same for line 2, where the second No column field, Course Number2, has a value of 2, finding the matching course record and placing its contents upon the screen as demanded by the relationship named Course2 . . . and so on.

Now for the fields on the line beginning Course 1 2 3 4 5. There are five fields upon this line, one for each course (see how things are beginning to get rigid – hard coded – around the idea of five courses?). They are simple one-character text fields that are to be named in sequence No1, No2, No3, No4 and No5. Allow data entry for these fields. The concept here is that if a student wants to attend course number 2, then they will set the box labelled number 2 to Y. If they also require course number 5, then box 5 will also need to be set to Y. The boxes directly relate to the courses they are numbered after. Were someone to complete boxes 1 and 2 because there are two courses they want to receive, our procedure will assume they require courses 1 and 2, even though that might not be the true situation.

Designing this screen is probably the trickiest bit of the whole Control procedure routine. So don't be afraid to spend some time getting it right. Once you are happy with it, move on to write its accompanying code.

The Registration procedure starts with the ever present global declaration for the field Student ID. This is required in order for DataEase to know which student we are interested in. However, we don't require the Run Status flag field. That was only of interest to the Control procedure Registration TP, so that can be safely ignored from now on.

```
define global "STUDENT ID" Numeric String 4 .
```

The procedure is required to create a Student Courses record for each course the student is going to attend. These records require some information from the student's Student form, namely surname, title and christian names. Therefore we need to link these two forms. This code will achieve that for us:

```
For STUDENT with Student Number = global STUDENT ID ;
```

In English this instructs DataEase to find a Student record with the same Student Number as that held in the global variable named Student ID.

```
If data-entry NO1 = "Y" then
    enter a record in STUDENT COURSES
        Student Number := global STUDENT ID ;
        TITLE := STUDENT TITLE ;
        CHRISTIAN NAMES := STUDENT CHRISTIAN NAMES ;
        SURNAME := STUDENT SURNAME ;
        COURSE NUMBER := 1;
        COURSE TITLE := data-entry COURSE TITLE1 .
end
```

Here we've made use of a conditional statement to find out if box number 1, named No1, on the data-entry screen has been set to Y. It defaults to Blank. If it has then a Student Courses record is created for course number 1 using a mix mash of data from the screen and the Student record. If the No1 field had been left unset, then no such record would be created for this course number. The remaining code for this procedure follows the same pattern, only setting up a Student Courses record for a course number if its box on the screen has been set to Y.

The full code listing is as follows:

```
define global "STUDENT ID" Numeric String 4 .

for STUDENT with Student Number = global STUDENT ID ;

If data-entry NO1 = "Y" then
    enter a record in STUDENT COURSES
        Student Number := global STUDENT ID ;
        TITLE := STUDENT TITLE ;
        CHRISTIAN NAMES := STUDENT CHRISTIAN NAMES ;
        SURNAME := STUDENT SURNAME ;
        COURSE NUMBER := 1;
        COURSE TITLE := data-entry COURSE TITLE1 .
end

If data-entry NO2 = "Y" then
    enter a record in STUDENT COURSES
        Student Number := global STUDENT ID ;
        TITLE := STUDENT TITLE ;
        CHRISTIAN NAMES := STUDENT CHRISTIAN NAMES ;
        SURNAME := STUDENT SURNAME ;
        COURSE NUMBER := 2;
        COURSE TITLE := data-entry COURSE TITLE2 .
end

If data-entry NO3 = "Y" then
    enter a record in STUDENT COURSES
        Student Number := global STUDENT ID ;
        TITLE := STUDENT TITLE ;
        CHRISTIAN NAMES := STUDENT CHRISTIAN NAMES ;
        SURNAME := STUDENT SURNAME ;
        COURSE NUMBER := 3;
        COURSE TITLE := data-entry COURSE TITLE3 .
end

If data-entry NO4 = "Y" then
    enter a record in STUDENT COURSES
        Student Number := global STUDENT ID ;
        TITLE := STUDENT TITLE ;
        CHRISTIAN NAMES := STUDENT CHRISTIAN NAMES ;
        SURNAME := STUDENT SURNAME ;
        COURSE NUMBER := 4;
        COURSE TITLE := data-entry COURSE TITLE4 .
end

If data-entry NO5 = "Y" then
    enter a record in STUDENT COURSES
        Student Number := global STUDENT ID ;
        TITLE := STUDENT TITLE ;
        CHRISTIAN NAMES := STUDENT CHRISTIAN NAMES ;
        SURNAME := STUDENT SURNAME ;
        COURSE NUMBER := 5;
        COURSE TITLE := data-entry COURSE TITLE5 .
end

end
```

Remember to save this procedure as Registration before loading up the procedure that we've already written named Student Liability. Originally this DQL code read every Student record on file, calculated the student's course liability, and then updated the Student record accordingly. This procedure now has to be amended such as to make the code only handle a specific student, namely the one identified by the global variable Student ID. Fortunately this code only requires a very minor amendment: The addition of the global variable definition and the alteration of the Student record search to make it student specific rather than general.

Accordingly the new code is to read:

```
define global "STUDENT ID" Numeric String 4 .
   define temp "RUNNING TOTAL" Number  .

for STUDENT with Student Number = global STUDENT ID ;
   assign temp RUNNING TOTAL := 0
   for STUDENT COURSES with ( Student Number = STUDENT Student Number )
      for COURSE with (COURSE NUMBER = STUDENT COURSES COURSE NUMBER)
         assign temp RUNNING TOTAL := temp RUNNING TOTAL + COURSE FEE
      end
   end
   modify records
      COURSE FEES := temp RUNNING TOTAL ;
      TOTAL CHARGED := temp RUNNING TOTAL + ENROLMENT FEE
end
```

That leaves just one further procedure to be amended before we can try running our Control procedure. Having recorded our new students' details and the courses they are to attend, the procedure above calculated the amount they need to pay the college, so all that remains to be done is the production of a detailed bill.

The body of the code we wrote earlier on in this chapter for the procedure named College Fees can be left to stand. But there is a requirement for some additional code to be written around it. The first piece being the ever-present global definition code:

```
define global "STUDENT ID" Numeric String 4 .
```

Then the code instructing DataEase to access every Student record has to be modified so that just the form belonging to our student is processed.

```
for STUDENT with Student Number = global STUDENT ID ;
```

Most of the code below the statement *list records ;* can be left alone, except that now that the Student record holds the total course bill (it was calculated by the previous procedure) there's no need to ask DataEase to do the work again, so remove the line that reads:

```
all COSTING COURSE FEE : sum .
```

Finally we need to act the meat of the report to the bill, namely the total course fees and the amount due to be paid. The first End statement in the code has caused the Student form to be reinstated as the prime form. Therefore all that is required is to add another listing command to have the fields holding this information displayed, thus:

```
list records
   COURSE FEES ;
   ENROLMENT FEE ;
   TOTAL CHARGE.
```

This is how the finished code is to look:

```
define global "STUDENT ID" Numeric STRING 4 .

for STUDENT with Student Number = global STUDENT ID ;
   for STUDENT COURSES
      with (Student Number = STUDENT Student Number)
         list records
            SURNAME in groups with group totals ;
            TITLE ;
            CHRISTIAN NAMES ;
            all COSTING COURSE TITLE in order ;
            all COSTING COURSE FEE .
   end

list records
   COURSE FEES ;
   ENROLMENT FEE ;
   TOTAL CHARGED.
```

The original reports were output to screen, and you will need to change this if you require the student's bill to be printed out. Once this procedure has been re-saved we will be ready to run our first Control procedure together. Load up the procedure we named Registration TP and start it running.

The Student Registration screen should first appear ready for a student's name and address details to be entered. We could go straight on and supply DataEase with the student details printed below. However, to test the <Esc> key detection code that we have included in our DQL, press that key now. You should be returned to the DQL menu screen. The flag variable Run Status has not been set to Continue and so the rest of the DQL code inside the Control procedure has been ignored. Start the procedure running again and this time provide the student details below.

```
Mr Dennis Hall     Age 40 +              Employment = Business


HOME          251 Access Way            Contacted = Word Of Mouth
              Billingham
              Hants                      Enrolment Fee = £25.00
              HA4 3XY

Courses =    Basic Computer Skills, English Literature and Physical
             Education
```

Press <F2> and the screen will go blank while the other procedures are run. You will see the name of each procedure appear in the top left-hand corner of the screen as it is loaded automatically. Once all the procedures detailed in the Control procedure have been completed you will be returned to the DQL menu screen. In case you want to try it again, here is another student's details for you record.

```
Mrs Kay Lewis      Age 40 +              Employment = Business

HOME          22 Lemmingside            Contacted = Radio Advert
              Canvas Town
              Hants                      Enrolment Fee = £25.00
              HL3 2AE

Courses =    Advanced Social Sciences,
             English Literature
```

If you've stuck with it, and completed all the exercises, well done. You'll probably be relieved to hear that there is now no further DQL code or data to be produced. Hopefully the work we've done together has helped you to learn the DataEase basics. Now go ahead and experiment on your own, you can't damage either your computer or DataEase. But you can lose valuable data so you'll need to take regular back-ups.

Back-ups, we've not discussed yet. This subject and other matters close to a database administrator's heart, such as access security and providing menu systems, you will find covered by the next chapter.

Other Users

Throughout this book occasional mention has been made of other people using your database. Called *users*, they now are now about to become the focus of our attention.

The problems faced by our users need to be appreciated. For one thing it would be very wrong for you to assume that they know as much about computers as you do. It might be the first time they've ever used one – remember how you felt before you touched a keyboard? It is not uncommon for people to worry about using a machine, afraid perhaps that they are going to cause it to blow a fuse just by touching it.

Accordingly your user needs reassurance and to be treated with kid gloves. Whenever I write a program, my imaginary target audience is always my grandmother. This isn't because she's particularly dense or anything like that. Far from it – in fact, she often whips off the answers to the Times crossword puzzle in a matter of minutes. But she does have a problem handling anything that requires buttons to be pushed – the remote control for the TV, or the microwave oven, for example. For some reason her mind just switches off when faced with anything from the silicon chip age. And an awful lot of people (from ALL age groups) have the same problem.

Therefore it would be a bit unkind to expect them to be able to navigate through DataEase's various menu systems as well as you can. They would probably feel far more comfortable if they just had to face a single menu screen. One from which they could run any, or all, of your carefully written DQL procedures. The facility to provide just such a menu system is available in DataEase.

In fact, this facility goes way beyond simply providing user-friendly menu screens. It also has some seriously heavy security implications as you will soon discover. Menus are set up via option 5, *Menu.Definition*, on DataEase's main menu.

Menu Definition

Whenever a user first logs into DataEase, the program checks to see if they have been assigned a particular Start Up menu. There is nothing really exciting about Start Up menus. They are simply the first menu that any individual user will encounter once inside the database software. If no such menu has been identified for that user, DataEase will cause the default menu (its own Main Menu) to be displayed.

Obviously we do not want too many of our users to be able to access that Main Menu. Imagine the damage (deliberate or otherwise) that someone familiar with DataEase could do if given the opportunity. Therefore, since users are restricted to just the functions provided by their menu, a Start Up menu can be used as an additional means of controlling database access. Users will not be aware of any processing outside those provided by their menu.

```
Menus
New Record on Screen
                          MENU DEFINITION
        MENU NAME  DATA ENTRY              SECURITY LEVEL Medium2

You can define up to 9 choices per menu, selected by digits 1 to 9.
Choice 0 always returns to the previous menu.

For each choice, provide the Choice Description and the Function Type.
Function Name is required for "user menu", "record entry" and "form reorg."
and optional for "data import", "program call", "procedure" and "install appl".
For "program call", Function Name may be continued into the next Description.

    MENU TITLE  PORTERHOUSE COLLEGE DATABASE - DATA ENTRY MENU
NO.        CHOICE DESCRIPTION           FUNCTION TYPE    FUNCTION NAME
1.RECORD NEW STUDENT                    procedure        REGISTRATION T.P
2.RECORD NEW LECTURER                   procedure        RECORD LECTURER
3.RECORD NEW COURSE                     procedure        RECORD COURSE DATA
4.ALLOCATE LECTURER TO COURSE           procedure        XREF LECTURER/COURSE
5.
6.
7.
8.
9.
F4CMDHELP ESCEXIT F2SAVE Sh-F1TABLE F3VIEW F7DEL F8MODIFY F9QBE F10MULTI
```

The menu definition screen

Above is the menu definition screen. Treat it simply as just another DataEase database form that has to be completed with some information. The first thing that we are required to provide is a name for the menu. The name that you choose identifies this particular menu to DataEase. When we come to set up our user definition later on, it is this name that we will use to identify the Start Up menu. As our example is to provide access to all the procedures that update the database information, let us call it *Data Entry*.

We are next asked what Security Level needs to be applied to the menu. We met security levels (user access levels) in Chapter 2 where we were told that seven exist. Table 8.1 details the various minimum security levels that a user requires in order to be allowed to perform certain DataEase functions. Remember, however, that these are subject to any other security restriction you apply. In addition it should not be assumed that just because a user can access a certain menu, that they can also use all the functions provided by that menu.

For example, should a user with an access rating of Low 1, be using a menu with a security rating of Low 2 (access levels allow processing at and below the level allocated) and attempt to select an option from that menu that requires a rating of High 1, they would be refused access to that processing even though it is listed as being available upon the menu.

Table 8.1: Minimum security levels

DataEase Function	High	Medium			Low		
	1	1	2	3	1	2	3
Define Menus	Y	N	N	N	N	N	N
Define Users	Y	N	N	N	N	N	N
Define/Modify Forms	Y	N	N	N	N	N	N
Define/Modify Relationships	Y	N	N	N	N	N	N
View Relationships	Y	Y	Y	Y	Y	Y	Y
Define/Modify Procedures	Y	N	N	N	N	N	N
Use Procedures	Y	Y	Y	Y	Y	Y	Y
View Records	Y	Y	Y	Y	Y	Y	Y
Back-up Database	Y	Y	Y	Y	Y	Y	Y
Restore Database	Y	N	N	N	N	N	N

If no Security Access is defined for a menu DataEase automatically defaults it to a value of Low 3. Our menu should be given a security access level of Medium 2.

Having accomplished that, we next need to supply a menu title. The one keyed here will appear as a banner heading upon the screen every time the menu is displayed, so choose with some care. In this case we'll use the title: *Porterhouse College Database – Data Entry Menu.*

The cursor will now move down the screen, entering a table area. Here we can describe the functions that are to be provided by the menu. The table is split into three columns. The first, headed *Choice Description*, is used to describe a menu item. The narrative text that we provide here will appear upon the menu screen. Therefore it needs to portray accurately the action with which it is to be associated. Even more important, it needs to be meaningful to the user. Each description can be up to 44 characters long and they will be displayed upon the menu in the same order as you record them in the table.

The first processing that we are going to describe upon our data-entry menu is the control DQL procedure that we wrote earlier named Registration TP. Remember, it records new student details, using such information as their name and address. It also notes the courses they are going to attend. The title *Record New Student* seems a suitable, meaningful description of that processing, so type that into the first column. Then press <Enter> to move across to the next column, that's headed *Function Type*.

There are 15 function types available, here's a brief description of each:

Main Menu
Provides access to DataEase's own main menu.

User Menu
Used to link screens. Say, for example, you had too many processing options to fit onto a single menu screen.The only course of action open to you in such circumstances is to set up another menu that contains the remaining options. It can then be called from within the first menu via this function. *Full Menu*, described later in this chapter, makes use of this function.

Record Entry
Causes a form's Record Entry screen to be displayed. This method of data entry was detailed in Chapter 3.

Query
Will result in the DQL menu screen being displayed. Any of the options upon that menu will then become available for selection, subject, of course, to the user's security level.

Procedure
Prompts the procedure named in the Function Name column to be run.

Status
This provides direct access to a menu option that appears on the Maintenance Menu which is described later inside this chapter. Briefly, Status causes a count of the number of records associated with each Form Type to be reported.

Backup
Enables a security backup of the entire database to be conducted.

Restore
Allows the data stored as a backup to be put back onto the database.

Utilities   Another direct route to a menu – this time it's the Utilities menu where such tasks as data import can be carried out.

Data Import   Automatically provides a means of directly accessing the Data Import function aboard the Utilities menu.

Program Call   Enables a program outside DataEase to be run directly from a menu.

Form Reorg   Causes the form specified in the Function Name column to be re-organised, i.e. to have records marked for deletion actually removed from the database. See Chapter 2 for more details.

Lock DB/Unlock DB   This provides a direct method of locking and unlocking the database. If your database is on a network there will be occasions when you require the database to be locked to prevent other people from accessing it while you are updating a record. It can be disregarded if you are not using DataEase upon a network.

Install Appli   Short for Install Application. It is possible that you might wish to move databases (applications) around DataEase environments. For example you might have built up a large amount of information upon your database that someone else would like to use within their DataEase program. This function provides a means of copying your database DQL code, forms and data.

```
 ┌──────────────────────────────────────────────────────────────────┐
 │  DataEase                                                          │
 │                                                                    │
 │                                                                    │
 │        ┌───────────────────────────────────────────────────┐      │
 │        │ PORTERHOUSE COLLEGE DATABASE - DATA RETRIEVAL MENU │      │
 │        │                                                    │      │
 │        │   1. LIST LECTURERS NAMES & ADDRESSES              │      │
 │        │                                                    │      │
 │        │   2. DISPLAY COLLEGE CURRICULUM                    │      │
 │        │                                                    │      │
 │        │   3. DISPLAY STUDENT NAMES & ADDRESSES             │      │
 │        │                                                    │      │
 │        │   4. DISPLAY STUDENTS COURSES                      │      │
 │        │                                                    │      │
 │        │   5. DISPLAY CONTACT REPORT                        │      │
 │        │  ═ 1 to 5 ═ UP ═ DOWN ═ RETURN ═ END ═             │      │
 │        └───────────────────────────────────────────────────┘      │
 │                                                                    │
 └──────────────────────────────────────────────────────────────────┘
```

Data Retrieval menu screen

The function type needed by our menu option Record New Student is number <5>, Procedure. This is because we wish a DQL procedure to be automatically run in response to this menu option being selected. It is the name of this procedure that we are next prompted to supply, as the cursor skips across to the third and last column. Headed *Function Name*, this column holds the names of the procedures that are to be used. Accordingly it is here that we need to enter the name of our Control procedure *Registration TP*. Once that has been done we can press <Enter> to move down to the next line.

That's the first menu line built. When the menu is displayed, its first option will now read:

1 – Record New Student

And then all our user needs to do, is press the <1> key in order to start the Registration TP procedure running. No complicated navigation through the DataEase menus. No loading of procedures, just the simple pressing of a single key. See, we can make life as easy for our user as DataEase makes it for us!

There are a few more functions to be added to this menu, and their details are listed below, so please enter them onto the menu definition form. Once that job has been completed, press <F2> to save the menu's definition onto the database.

Choice Description	Function Type	Function Name
Record New Lecturer	<5> – Procedure	Record Lecturer
Record New Course	<5> – Procedure	Record Course Data
Allocate Lecturer to Course	<5> – Procedure	XRef Lecturer/Course

The Porterhouse database requires four menu screens in all, and so far we've only described the first. The others are to be named Data Access, Basic Access and Full Access. The information required to describe these menus is contained below. Press <F3> now to clear the form area and then enter the required data for each menu. Please be careful to note their different security access levels.

You may notice that the last menu screen (Full Access) only contains calls to other menu screens. It has been provided for YOU to use as the database administrator. There will be times when you will want to access the database as a normal user, hence the provision of the first two options. But you may also need to use the DataEase menu so why not benefit from a menu screen yourself?

Basic Access Menu description

Name = Basic Access   Security Level = Low 1
Title = Porterhouse College Database – Information

Choice Description	Function Type	Function Name
Display College Curriculum	Procedure	List Courses

Data Access Menu description

Name = Data Access   Security Level = Medium 1

Title = Porterhouse College Database – Data Retrieval Menu

Choice Description	Function Type	Function Name
Display Lecturer's		
Names & Addresses	Procedure	List Lecturers
Display College Curriculum	Procedure	List Courses
Display Students'		
Names & Addresses	Procedure	Display Student Data
Display Contact Report	Procedure	Contact Report

Full Access Menu description

Name = Full Access   Security Level = High 1

Title = Porterhouse College Database

Choice Description	Function Type	Function Name
Data Retrieval	User Menu	Data Access
Data Update	User menu	Data Entry
DataEase Main Menu	Main Menu	

Note: The main menu does not require a function name to be provided.

User Definition

How does a user get permission to use your database? Chapter 2 spent some time describing the DataEase logging on screen. Special mention was made of the fact that if DataEase did not recognise the name and passwords supplied, it would refuse access. To date, the only person it will allow to use the database is you. Unless that is, you've let slip your login script (computerspeak phrase for the names and passwords you provide to log onto DataEase).

This means that you are the only person able to benefit from all the code and information you've keyed. If that's what you want, then there's no problem. If it's not, then security issues aside, you've got a major flaw to overcome. How can DataEase be persuaded to allow other people to use your database, while still preserving data security?

The answer lies within User Definitions. Everybody including yourself, as you will discover in a moment, who can access a database will have had some information recorded about them by DataEase. This data is held upon a form called the User Definition.

Select option <7>, *System Administration,* from the DataEase Main Menu screen and then option <1>, *Define Users,* from the resultant menu screen. You should now be looking at a User Definition form. Press <F3> and your own user description will be displayed. The record was written when you first logged into DataEase.

```
┌─────────────────────────────────────────────────────────────────────┐
│  Users                                                                │
│  New Record on Screen                                                 │
│                                                                       │
│                         USER INFORMATION                              │
│                         ─────────────────                             │
│                                                                       │
│         Name         : RICHARD NWANZE                                 │
│                                                                       │
│         Password     : SAMMY                                          │
│                                                                       │
│         Level        : Medium2                                        │
│                                                                       │
│         Screen Style :                                                │
│                        Leave blank for system provided default styles.│
│                                                                       │
│         Start-up Menu : DATA ENTRY                                    │
│                         Leave blank to use system provided menus.     │
│                                                                       │
│         Help Level   :                                                │
│                        Leave blank to provide help on demand.         │
│                                                                       │
│  F4CMDHELP ESCEXIT F2SAVE Sh-F1TABLE F3VIEW F7DEL F8MODIFY F9QBE F10MULTI │
└─────────────────────────────────────────────────────────────────────┘
```

User Definition screen

Every entry upon this screen can be amended if you wish. The first three field names are pretty self explanatory but what about the remainder?. Let's discuss screen style first.

DataEase can appear in many formats to the user. You are able to control exactly which colours are to appear upon the screens, perhaps switching the background and foreground around, or maybe highlighting a particular area of the screen for a special effect. This is achieved by defining a screen style.

Any number of these can be defined, so if you wished, every user of your database could be allocated different colour screens and text styles. This facility can be used just for fun, or for a more serious purpose, it's up to you! So how do you go about setting up a screen style?

By now it's likely that you are getting used to DataEase's little ways and means. So there should be only a mild reaction when you learn that screen styles are described on yet another DataEase form. It is accessed via option <4>, *Define Screen Styles,* on the Administration menu. The Screen Style has first to be allocated a unique name, which can then be supplied to this User Definition form in field number 4. The remainder of the screen consists of choice fields, requiring only that you select the colour that you want to be used within the area described.

Foreground   The colour of the text.

Background   The colour of the screen.

Intensify   If set to Yes will cause the colour of the text to be intensified, such that the text will be highlighted upon the screen. Warning – Intensified Brown will appear as Yellow, while Light Gray will show as White.

Blink   Text can be made to flash upon the screen. If this is required, perhaps for an error message, then set this field to Yes.

This diagram shows whereabouts each screen area can be found:

```
┌─────────────────────────────────────────────────────────────┐
│ TITLE AREA          MODE AREA            MESSAGE AREA        │
│ PROMPT LINE                                                  │
├─────────────────────────────────────────────────────────────┤
│                                                              │
│                                                              │
│                                                              │
│                                                              │
│                     DISPLAY AREA                             │
│                                                              │
│                     Regular Fields                           │
│                     Highlight 1                              │
│                     Highlight 2                              │
│                     Highlight 3                              │
│                     Menu Highlighting                        │
│                     Key Names                                │
│                     All Other                                │
│                                                              │
│                                                              │
├─────────────────────────────────────────────────────────────┤
│                  FUNCTION KEY LINE                           │
└─────────────────────────────────────────────────────────────┘
```

The DataEase screen colour area locations

Their default colours are as follows:

Description	Text	Background
Regular	Yellow	Blue
Highlight 1	White	Red
Highlight 2	Yellow	Black
Highlight 3	Black	Black
Title area	Yellow	Black
Mode area	Cyan	Black
Message area	Red	Black
Prompt line	Black	Green
Menu highlight	White	Blue
Key names	White	Red
Normal	Yellow	Black

Once you've decided upon your screen effects, simply save the form by pressing <F2> and it will then be available to be used upon a User Definition form, being named within the field labelled Screen Style.

The next field upon the User Definition form refers to the Start Up menu that that users will be presented with when they first log onto DataEase. Amend this now to read *Full Access*, the name of the menu screen to be used by the System Administrator (you) that we described just a little while back. Now, the next time you enter DataEase, it won't be the menu screen that you've become so used to that you will see first, but the Full Access menu instead.

Finally we are asked what level of help is appropriate to the user being defined. There is a choice of two settings. The default value is *On Demand*, and requires the user to press <Alt> and <F1> in order to be provided with some assistance. The other value is that of *Automatically* which means that DataEase will routinely display any Help message that you have defined (remember Form design in Chapter 2?) as the user accesses a form or field. Its own System Help messages will still only appear in response to keys <Alt> and <F1> being pressed.

As with all DataEase forms, pressing <F2> will result in the User Definition form being saved onto the database. However, as your details have already been recorded, press <F8>, *Modify*, instead, so that your user Definition form can be updated with the new information upon the screen.

In order to give you an opportunity to practice defining users, below are the names of some other people who are keen to be allowed to use your Porterhouse database.

Name	Password	Level	Menu
Richard Nwanze	SAMMY	Medium 2	Data Entry
Chris Bates	SHRIMPER	Medium 1	Data Access
Colin Pearson	QUALITY	Low 1	Basic Access

Once you've defined those users, log completely out of DataEase. Then re-enter, each time assuming a different personality, and see what happens.

Housekeeping and Other Fun Tasks

Put away any images you might be having of brushes and mops, I'm not going to be discussing the arduous task of keeping a house neat and tidy. As my wife will only too unhappily confirm, I am expert at only the reverse.

No, what I am referring to here are the odd jobs that fall the way of the database administrator from time to time. Some are extremely important and must not under any circumstances be skipped, while others can perhaps be treated more casually.

We'll kick off with the most important job you are going to be faced with once your database is up and running, namely Data Archiving. Now, it doesn't matter how careful you are with your computer. You can polish it and call it nice names every morning – it won't make the slightest bit of difference. One day, as certain as the arrival of a winter's fuel bill, your machine is going to do a nasty. Depending upon its personality, it might wait until the day that you really need it, or maybe it will let you down gently once all the annual accounts have been completed. But break down it will, be absolutely certain of that.

Accept that, and you are already over halfway to retrieving the situation before it occurs. Why? Because you will have recognised the need to take out insurance – in the form of regular data archives. These are simply copies of your database code AND data that are held somewhere other than upon your computer. The usual practice is to copy all your database information down onto a floppy disk which is then stored away somewhere secure. Fireproof safes immediately leap to mind as an excellent choice.

In case you think I am over emphasising the situation, pause for a moment to think how much work you've put into the Porterhouse database. If all that code were to be lost because your hard drive decided to call it a day, would you cheerfully turn back to Chapter 2 and start all over again? How much easier life would be if you'd taken a copy of the database and stored it upon a floppy disk. Within minutes your database could be up and working on another machine. Think about it.

How often you take archiving action is up to you. It depends upon various factors, including how important the data is, how often it's updated, and its volume. While writing this book I've archived its text after every session at the keyboard.

Lecture over, now here's some instruction on how to set about creating a data archive of your database. First of all access the Maintenance menu via option 6, *Database Maintenance*, from the DataEase Main Menu. This maintenance menu has lots of goodies on it.

1 – Database Status

This menu option provides you with a means of accessing such information as the DOS file names applied to your database forms and procedures. The report displayed (or it can be output to a printer if you prefer) details each DataEase form/procedure's name along with its size and DOS title. In addition, where forms are being reported, it will also supply statistics concerning the number of existing and deleted records owned by the form.

2 – Backup Database

Backup or archive, the term used doesn't really matter, it's the action performed that is all important. To demonstrate how to implement a database archive we are going to backup our Porterhouse database now.

Select this option from the menu, and a box will appear at the base of the screen. It will contain a prompt requesting you to:

Specify the Path name to use for backup and press Return.

DataEase is simply wishing to know where you want it to copy your database to. Although it will happily copy your DQL code and data into another directory upon your computer, this would be a bit self defeating. When your machine decides it's time to call it a day, it's going to destroy everything on your hard disk, not just the DEASE directory.

Therefore it is much more sensible to archive your database to floppy. So place a clean, formatted, disk in Drive A. Then tell DataEase that is where you want the database copied to by typing the drive letter *A:* in response to its question.

DataEase will then display a rather unnerving message that reads:

If a backup error occurs, what do you want to do?

Don't worry, it is just being cautious. You have the choice of three responses:
 1 – Ignore error and continue
 2 – Cancel
 3 – Decide upon error

Opting for answer 1 would be a bit gung-ho. Suppose the error has arisen because you've failed to insert the disk properly? Answer 2 is a bit safer, although if the problem was only caused by a mis-aligned disk you could be over reacting slightly by aborting the whole backup procedure. Therefore I tend to favour option 3 in this situation. Should a real problem arise you can easily cancel the action before it does any damage. Alternatively you can solve the problem, in this case by pushing the disk properly into place, and then continue with the archiving action.

DataEase will now prepare to start the archiving procedure. But before it does so, it will first check back with you to confirm that the database is still to be backed up,displaying the message:

Starting Backup – press Return when ready or 'ESC' to Abort.

Respond by pressing <Enter>. Once the action has started, DataEase continuously reports how the backup is progressing. It starts with the forms, the name of each being displayed as it is copied, and then moves onto the DQL Procedures. Once the archive has been completed a screen message will appear displaying the time and date the database was copied.

Proceed by following DataEase's instruction to again press <Enter> and it will then report that the Backup has been completed. Press <Enter> a final time to be returned to the maintenance menu screen.

3 – Restore Database

Via this menu option an archived database can be copied back into DataEase. A point to be aware of when taking this action concerns any new or amended information that you may have recorded upon the database since the backup was taken. It will all disappear, just as if it had never existed at all. This is because, as far as DataEase is concerned, you've turned the clock back to the time and date you made the archive. It will forget any action you've taken since then.

4 – Operating System Functions (DOS Functions on versions before DataEase 4.5)

An extremely useful menu option this one, as it allows you to exit temporarily from DataEase and return to the DOS environment. Some of the more common DOS commands can be directly accessed via this menu.

1 – Data Disk Directory
Provides a file listing of the DEASE directory, a screen at a time.
2 – Check Data Disk
Performs the DOS CHKDSK command on the C: Drive.
3 – Format New Disk
Allows you to format a disk, perhaps before using it as an archive disk.
4 – DOS Backup
Enables you to backup files from one disk to another.
5 – DOS Restore
Allows you to bring them back again.

6 – Other

If the DOS command(s) you wish to use are not covered by the menu, this option will place you inside the DOS environment. Once there you can play with whichever DOS commands you require. But remember to return to DataEase, by typing *Exit*, once your need for DOS has been satisfied. Should you not do so, your database could become corrupted.

5 – Lock Database

If you are working inside a network environment it is possible to lock your database to prevent other people from accessing it. You might wish to do this because you are working on sensitive data or perhaps conducting a major update to the database.

6 – Unlock Database

Once the need to keep other people frozen out of your database has gone, you need some means of unlocking it. Hence the provision of this command.

Utilities Menu

Another menu that you may wish to access from time to time is the Utilities Menu. It is reached via option 5, *Database Utilities*, on the Administration menu.

1 – Import

Via this menu option it is possible to import, to the current database, some data from a source external to DataEase.

2 – Transfer Data

This menu option is used to copy the data recorded upon one DataEase form into another. It is important to note that data will only be transferred between fields with the same name, i.e. fields intended to receive information on the second form must have names that are identical to their data source fields on the original.

3 – Install Form

This menu option is used to copy into the current database, a form described upon another DataEase database. Remember, the DOS filenames etc are available via option 1, *Database Status*, on the Maintenance menu.

4 – Install Procedure

As with the above menu option, this provides a means of copying into your current database, data from another DataEase database. In this case the information made available for transfer consists of DQL procedures.

5 – Install Application

Effectively the processing made available by this menu option combines those provided by options 2, 3 and 4 above. In other words it allows you to copy an entire database into DataEase.

6 – Change Database Name

After checking your name and password credentials this option provides the facility for you to rename your database.

7 – Remove Database

Be very certain about what you want to do before selecting this menu option, because it enables you to delete the entire current database. Once removed, the database cannot be recovered. So be very careful!

DataEase for Windows

In November 1992 DataEase International released a new version of DataEase. Named DataEase Express, it was the first DataEase database program to be specifically written to be fully compatible with the Windows operating system environment. Versions 4.5 and above of the DOS software could be used with Windows but it was not possible for them to exploit the operating system's facilities to the full. DataEase Express has no such restrictions.

While it is beyond the scope of this guide to provide detailed information about this new program and its many exciting facilities, I will try to give you a brief taste of what it has to offer.

First of all, forget any ideas you might have about it being simply an upgraded version of DataEase with a few extra bells and whistles thrown in for good measure. It is a completely fresh product that, if marketed under another name, would not be immediately recognised as being a member of the DataEase family. That is not to say that all the best practices of the DOS programs have been abandoned or forgotten. They are still very much in evidence and the software is just as much fun to get along with as the DataEase products described in this book.

If you now feel able to work with DataEase there is no need to be fearful about tackling DataEase Express. If you are one of those people who just doesn't like Windows (you've plenty of company if that is the case) you can also abandon any worries about DataEase International ceasing to support its DOS products. DataEase Version 4.53 has just been released and other versions are planned for the future.

From the moment the first DataEase Express screen is displayed you become aware that you are inside a totally new environment. Colours and pictures abound, especially if you access one of the many example databases provided. One of the most colourful is named Club ParaDEASE. This database is used primarily as a teaching aid, but its secondary purpose is to show you just what DataEase Express is capable of.

Colours and Fonts

One of the lesser qualities of DataEase, as you've already discovered in this book, is its inability to provide screen reports that show field values in different colours. This problem has been addressed by the Windows version, and how!

Not only can individual fields be allocated disparate colours, but their text can now also appear in a number of sizes and fonts. Screen design has become an art form. This has its dangers as well as its benefits because budding Andy Warhols will have a field day mixing colour combinations together, but please remember your users.

Allocating colour and font characteristics to a field is a very simple process. Click on the field in question – yes click – it's a Windows program so you need a mouse, and a pop-up menu will appear that contains three options: Definition, Display and Font. Click on Display, and a Display Attributes screen will appear.

On this screen are a number of colours to choose from, 16 to be exact, but if you require more, then a simple click within the box labelled *More Colours* will result in a colour chart being displayed that holds some 48 colours. It also provides you with the opportunity to pick and mix colours to obtain another 16 possible combinations. You then only have to decide which of the 64 possible colours to allocate to your field's background. Of course, once that's out of the way, you've then got to make a decision concerning the colour of the text.

When you've finished playing around with the colour characteristics of your field it's time to start considering its font. A font describes how the text is to appear upon the screen, in *italics* for example. Click on the font button and the font screen will appear. Three menu lists immediately strike your eye. One contains a list of the names of possible fonts, another concerns the style of the font (bold, regular etc.) while the last governs the actual size of the printed text. You can experiment with selections from each of these menus, a sample display of how your text will actually appear being shown upon the screen.

If you are like me, you'll be spending hours designing your screen displays. Fun? Certainly not – it's very hard work designing a database.

Pictures

I was not misleading you earlier when I mentioned pictures being used by DataEase Express. Not satisfied with giving you lots of colours and fonts to enjoy, DataEase International have also provided the facility for your database to store and display graphics.

Some are provided for you with the software package, but you are free to add others as you will. The database software will accept graphics in any of the formats .BMP, GIF, .WMF, .PCX, .EPS, .TIFF and .TGA.

Again it is a fairly straightforward business to have a graphic displayed by your database. Upon your form you draw a box around the area within which you wish your picture to appear, then you simply tell DataEase Express which graphic to use, in the same way as you might inform it of how long a text field is to be.

This facility means that now you can have photos of your staff appearing with their employment records, or perhaps instead, you'd rather have pictures of your product displayed along with some pertinent information. This way an advertising database could be set up that your customers could peruse by themselves.

It also means that your user interface can be much enhanced. For example, consider this situation in a theatre booking office. A customer wishes to book four seats for a performance and the booking is to be recorded upon a database. On one hand the screen display could just show the seat row and position reference numbers J9, 10, 11 and 12 perhaps – informative to those in the know but not over user friendly. Alternatively an actual display of the theatre could appear upon the screen with the seats in question highlighted. The customer can then see immediately where they are to be seated and so can the clerk, allowing any problems to be resolved at that point, rather than on the day they arrive for the performance.

OLE

Not Olé as in Spanish but OLE as in Object Linking and Embedding protocol. It's a Windows term so don't blame DataEase. What OLE allows you do is to pass information to another program that's running within Windows, such as a spreadsheet like Excel, have that program process the data to produce a graph or pie chart, and then receive that graphic report back into DataEase Express, ready to be displayed upon the screen. This means that screen displays can be updated in flight with information that's been provided by other programs.

Previously you will have been able to have an external program produce a graph based upon information contained by a DataEase database but you will not have been able to have that graph displayed by DataEase. Sales figures reports etc., could be much enhanced by this facility.

Multiple Forms

The present DOS DataEase program only allows you to have a maximum of two forms displayed upon the screen at any one time – the parent form and its subforms. DataEase Express, however, is able to let you show as many as you wish.

Therefore, were a customer's name and address details to be held upon one form, with order information on another and account details spread over billing and payment forms, all this information could be accessed via one screen. It provides a much tighter means of presenting data. Data entry also benefits as well.

Memo Field Property

An additional field type property named Memo (the others Text, Numeric String, Number, Date, Time, Pound, Yes/No and Choice you met in Chapter 2) has been made available. Basically it describes a text field that can store up to 4,000 descriptive characters, these being alpha or numeric, but not the wild card characters *, ? and ~.

This could be very usefully applied to describe a product.

DDE

Another Windows bit of terminology, DDE stands for Dynamic Data Exchange. Basically it enables you automatically to pass data out of DataEase Express across to a Windows word processor such as Ami Pro or Word for Windows. These programs can then act upon that information to produce letters etc. Obviously, each Windows program interacts with DDE differently so you will need to read the target program's documentation as well as DataEase Express's in order to have the data connection established correctly.

Foreign Databases

The final additional facility provided by DataEase Express is the ability to handle information provided by other databases such as Paradox and dBase. This allows an organisation that has a number of databases, each built using a different software package, to unite its data under one roof should it ever require to do so. Alternatively it could continue to keep the information apart but occasionally introduce it to DataEase Express in order to have a particular report produced. A very handy facility whichever way it's used.

DataEase Express will also accept data from DOS DataEase databases, although it is only fully compatible with versions 4.53 and above. Such databases can also accept data from their Windows cousin, so information can be freely exchanged between the two environments.

10

DataEase Commands

This chapter lists the DataEase DQL commands and their syntax. Some of them you will have already encountered during your passage through the guide. Others, however, will be new to you. Accordingly, where possible, examples of their usage are also provided.

ABS

ABS means absolute value. It's a mathematical function that converts a numeric value into a positive unsigned value. Numbers are usually preceded by a sign (+ or –) that indicates whether the value is positive or negative. Unsigning a value simply means removing this sign. In effect it makes the value positive. ABS must only be used with numeric fields – any string expression will result in a value of zero.

Usage: A DQL report contains two columns, one to hold credit data, the other debit information. The values for each column are calculated by DataEase. As the debit column is clearly labelled as being such there is no requirement for its figures to be preceded by a minus sign. Accordingly the ABS command could be used. It works thus:

Debit value = – 150

ABS (Debit value) = 150

```
Define Temp "ABSOLUTE VALUE" numeric 3.
    For ACCOUNTS ;
        assign temp ABSOLUTE VALUE := ABS (DEBIT VALUE) .
        list records
            TRANSACTION ;
            CREDIT VALUE ;
            temp ABSOLUTE VALUE.
```

ACOS

This is a trigonometric function that is used to calculate the arccosine of a numeric value, its result being expressed in radians between 0 and PI. The value provided to the function must be in the range −1 to 1. Anything outside that range is liable to cause your computer to seize up, unless you have a maths coprocessor installed.

Usage: RADIANS := ACOS (field name)

ALL

This command is used as a relational operator. It enables every record in a related form that matches the current record to be processed.

Usage: A relationship named Index exists between two forms named Item and Catalogue. You wish to process all the Item forms that are associated with a particular Catalogue form. The DQL code below tells DataEase to:

❑ Read a Catalogue form

❑ List a product's name and description

❑ Find all the Item forms that match the Index relationship criteria and report their sale information.

```
For CATALOGUE ;
   List Records
      PRODUCT in order ;
      DESCRIPTION ;
      all INDEX DATE SOLD in order ;
      all INDEX QUANTITY .
```

AMPM

This is a Time function that considers a value held in 24-hour format (HH.MM.SS) and returns its appropriate 12-hour time setting e.g. am or pm.

Example:

The instruction:

```
NOON RELATIONSHIP := AMPM (12:12:34)
```

would set the field named Noon Relationship to **pm** while the command:

```
NOON RELATIONSHIP := AMPM (05.06.23)
```

would cause it to have a setting of **am**

AND

This logical operator combines two sets of selection criteria. When used, a record has to satisfy all the specified selection criteria in order to be processed.

Example:

If only Catalogue records relating to yellow boots are required then AND would be used inside the DQL procedure thus:

```
For CATALOGUE
with PRODUCT = BOOTS and DESCRIPTION = YELLOW ;
   List Records
```

Accordingly DataEase would only select Catalogue records where the Product field held a value of Boots AND the Description field had a setting of Yellow. Any other combination of field values would cause a record to be ignored.

ANY

Another relational operator. This causes DataEase to select the first record in a relationship that matches the current record to be processed.

Usage: A relationship named Index exists between two forms named Item and Catalogue. You wish to obtain the value held within a field named Price on an Item form that is associated with a particular Catalogue form. The DQL code below tells DataEase to:

❑ Read a Catalogue form

❑ List a product's name and description

❑ Find the first (and only the first) Item form that matches the Index relationship criteria and report the value of its Price field.

```
For CATALOGUE ;
   List Records
      PRODUCT in order ;
      DESCRIPTION ;
      any INDEX PRICE .
```

So regardless of any other Item form that might meet the requirements of the Index relationship, only the first such record's data will be presented in the report.

ASIN

A Trigonometric function that calculates the arcsine of a numeric value, within the range −1 to 1, expressed as angle in radians.

Usage: RADIANS := ASIN (Field name)

ASSIGN

A procedural command that is used to set the value of a temporary or global field.

Usage: ASSIGN FIELD STATUS FIELD NAME := value .

Example:

A temporary field named Run Status is to be given a value of *OK*

```
assign temp RUN STATUS := "OK" .
```

ATAN

A Trigonometric function that calculates the arctangent of a numeric value, within the range –1 to 1, expressed as angle in radians.

Usage: RADIANS := ATAN (Field name)

ATAN2

A Trigonometric function that calculates the arctangent of a numeric value, divided by another. The result is an angle described in radians.

Usage: RADIANS := ATAN2 (Field name 1, Field name 2)

where Field name 1's value is divided by that of Field name 2.

BETWEEN

A comparison operator. It is used to define a value range.

Example:

All the Item forms whose Price field contains a value between £5 and £20 are to be reported.

```
for ITEM with PRICE between 5 to 20 ;
   list records
```

This DQL code will cause all the Item records with a value equal to or greater than 5 and less than or equal to 20 to be processed.

BLANK

A keyword that means *null*. A null value is unspecified and therefore should not be mistaken as meaning zero or space. It is the default value that DataEase assigns to fields that have not been allocated any specific value. It can therefore be used inside a DQL test condition as a means of discovering whether or not a specific field has been provided with a value by the user.

Example:

A field exists upon a data-entry screen named Credit Card. The user is required to set it to Y if a customer pays for goods with a piece of plastic. Otherwise it can be ignored – a situation that DataEase is required to recognise and react to by applying a value of Cash when the transaction is recorded upon the database.

When the screen is first displayed DataEase automatically defaults the fields setting to NULL. Therefore our DQL code can read:

```
If data-entry CREDIT CARD = BLANK then
   METHOD OF PAYMENT := "CASH" .
else
   METHOD OF PAYMENT := "CARD" .
end
```

BREAK

A procedural command that causes DataEase to immediately exit from inside a *for* or *while* command. Processing then continues from the first line outside the loop, if such exists.

Example:

A relationship named Index exists between two forms named Item and Catalogue. Only the first 20 Item forms that are associated with a particular Catalogue form are required to be reported. The DQL code below tells DataEase to:

❑ Read a Catalogue form

❑ List a product's name and description

❑ Find the first 20 Item forms that match the Index relationship criteria and report their sale information.

❑ Once 20 Item records have been reported, immediately abandon any further action.

```
For CATALOGUE ;
   List Records
      PRODUCT in order ;
      DESCRIPTION ;
      all INDEX DATE SOLD;
      all INDEX QUANTITY .
      if current item number > 20 then
         break
      end.
```

CASE

A conditional statement that can be used to replace an *If else* structure. (See Chapter 5 for more information)

Example:

```
Case (NAME)
   value "MARK"
      assign temp SPORT := "ANGLING" .
   value "SALLY"
      assign temp SPORT := "GYMKHANA" .
   value "TIM"
      assign temp SPORT := "FENCING" .
   value others
      assign temp SPORT := BLANK.

end
```

If the Namefield contains a value of Mark, Sally or Tim their sport is allocated to the temporary field named Sport. Any other names will cause that field to be allocated a null value.

CEIL

A mathematical function that rounds a numeric value up to the next integer value.

Usage: WHOLE NUMBER := CEIL (Field name)

If Field name = 2.5 then Whole Number will be given a value of 3.

COMPARISON SYMBOLS

These are used to compare one value with an other:

=	The values each side of the comparison symbol have to be *equal.*
<	The value on the right of the symbol has to be *higher than* the value on the left.
>	The value on the right of the symbol has to be *lower than* the value on the left.
<=	The value on the right of the symbol has to be *higher than* or *equal to* the value on the left.
>=	The value on the right of the symbol has to be *less than* or *equal to* the value on the left.
Between	The value has to be inside the range specified.
Not	Reverses the meaning of the comparison symbol.

Example: . . .

The command:

```
If DATE not = 01/04/93
```

means if the date equals anything other than 01/01/93.

COPY ALL FROM

A command that causes the values held by one form to be copied across into another. The data will only be copied from a form's field if an identically named field is present upon the receiving form.

Example:

Two forms are described thus upon a database:

Form 1	STAFF
	NAME
Fields	RANK
	OFFICE CODE
	SALARY
Form 2	OFFICE
	OFFICE CODE
Fields	NAME
	DESK
	RANK

Data has already been recorded upon the Staff forms but the Office forms have yet to be completed. Apart from the Desk field, all the remaining information they require is held upon a Staff form. Accordingly, this DQL code could be written to copy that information between the forms.

```
for STAFF ;
   enter a record in OFFICE
      OFFICE CODE = STAFF OFFICE CODE ;
      NAME = STAFF NAME ;
      RANK = STAFF RANK.
```

or alternatively the code could more easily be written as:

```
for STAFF ;
   enter a record in OFFICE
      COPY ALL FROM STAFF .
```

The saving in coding effort can be quite substantial where a situation demands that a lot of field content copying be done.

COS

A Trigonometric function that is used to calculate the cosine of an angle expressed in radians.

Usage: RADIANS := COS (Field name)

COSH

A Trigonometric function that is used to calculate the hyperbolic cosine of an angle in radians.

Usage: RADIANS := COSH (Field name)

COUNT

This operator maintains a count of the number of forms that are processed by a conditional DQL statement.

Example:

```
For STAFF with RANK = ACCOUNTANT ;
   list records
      NAME in order ;
      OFFICE CODE ;
      OFFICE CODE = 11 : Count .
end
```

This DQL code instructs DataEase to find all the Staff forms that are held for people with the rank of Accountant. Then display their names and office codes in alphabetical order. In addition it is also to report how many Accountants work in office number 11.

The report would look something like this:

Name	Office
Alan Curtis	12
Andy Edwards	14
Ian Gray	11
Keith Jones	11
Steve Phillips	12

Office 11 Total = 2

COUNT OF

A statistical operator that counts the number of *related* forms that are processed.

Example:

```
For OFFICE ;
   list records
      OFFICE CODE in order ;
      NAME in order ;
      any STAFF SALARY ;
      count of STAFF with (SALARY > 15000) .
end
```

This DQL code tells DataEase to process all the Office forms, reporting their codes in ascending order. The names of the staff within those offices are then to be detailed in alphabetical order, complete with their salary information. Finally a count is to be maintained of the number of staff with salaries over £15,000.

The subsequent report could look appear like this:

OFFICE 11

Ian Gray	14500
Keith Jones	25000

OFFICE 12

Alan Curtis	12000
Steve Phillips	22000

OFFICE 14

Andy Edwards	30000

No of Staff with Salary over £15,000 = 3

CURRENT

This is a keyword that is used to access the eight system controlled variables.

CURRENT DATE Returns the date held by the computer's internal clock. Adjusted by the DOS command DATE.

CURRENT TIME Returns the time as held by the computer's internal clock. Adjusted by the DOS command TIME.

CURRENT USER NAME Returns the name of the person currently using DataEase. The name appears as it was entered upon the login screen.

CURRENT USER LEVEL Returns the current user's security level i.e. HIGH 1

CURRENT PAGE NUMBER Returns the current page number of a multi-page report

CURRENT ITEM NUMBER Returns the number of the record currently being processed. See COUNT.

CURRENT COMPUTERNAME Used upon networks. It returns the name of the work station being used to access DataEase.

CURRENT STATUS Returns a numeric value that is determined according to what key a user has pressed while entering data using the DQL Input statement.

Key pressed	Action	Value
Esc	Exit	1
F2	Save	2
F8	Modify	3
F7	Delete	4

Example:

```
For STAFF ;
   List records
   NAME in order ;
   OFFICE ;
   CURRENT DATE.
end
```

A report generated by the above DQL code could appear like this:

DATE . . . 01/04/95	STAFF LIST
Name	**Office**
Alan Curtis	12
Andy Edwards	14
Ian Gray	11
Keith Jones	11
Steve Phillips	12

DATA-ENTRY

A keyword that identifies the data-entry screen as being the data source.

Example:

A data-entry screen contains fields Office and Name. The user is required to enter data into these fields before pressing <F2> to initiate the database update. This is how the DQL code needs to appear in order to record the information that's just been keyed onto the screen.

```
Enter a record in STAFF
   copy all from DATA-ENTRY .
```

This code will only work if the fields on the screen have identical names to fields that appear upon the target form, *COPY ALL* only working between fields that share a common name. Where screen fields have different names to those on the form, they have to be linked directly by the code, as in the example below:

```
Enter a record in STAFF
   NAME   := data entry SCREEN NAMEFIELD ;
   OFFICE := data entry SCREEN OFFICE CODE .
```

DATE
A date function command that builds up a date from three separate numbers.

Usage: DATEFIELD := date (DAY,MONTH,YEAR)

If DAY = 5, MONTH = 12, YEAR = 95 then Datefield will hold a value of 05/12/95.

DAY
This date function calculates the day of the month when provided with a date value.

Usage: DAYFIELD := day (DATE FIELD)

If Date Field held a value of 05/12/95 then Dayfield would be given a value of 5.

DEFINE
This command is required whenever a temporary or global field variable is being created. Such fields are used to hold values that might change or need calculating during a DQL procedure. Global variables can be used to pass values between procedures while temporary variables can only be used within their parent DQL code.

Example:

```
define temp "COUNTER" number .

for OFFICE ;
   assign temp COUNTER := temp COUNTER + 1 .
   list records
      OFFICE CODE.
end
```

Here a temporary variable named Counter has been set up as a number type field. As DataEase reports each office code value so the value of Counter is incremented by 1, its default start value being zero. It can then be used to report how many Office forms where processed. See also the COUNT command.

DELETE RECORDS

This DQL command causes records to be flagged for deletion from the database. A DataEase safety catch feature prevents records from physically being removed from the database until the owner form is re-organised. Chapter 2 refers.

Example:

```
For OFFICE with OFFICE CODE = 11 ;
   DELETE RECORDS
end
```

DataEase will search through the Office forms and flag for deletion all the records that are held with an Office Code value of 11.

DO

This keyword acts in partnership with the WHILE command. DataEase examines the WHILE condition and as long as the response is *TRUE* it will DO the actions contained within the WHILE command. As soon as a *FALSE* answer occurs an immediate exit will be made from the WHILE loop.

Example:

```
define temp "COUNTER" Number .

while temp COUNTER < 2 do
   For OFFICE ;
      assign temp COUNTER := temp COUNTER + 1 .
      list records
         OFFICE CODE .
   end

   end
```

The above DQL code instructs DataEase to:

❏ Set up a temporary variable named Counter

❏ Then while the value of the Counter field is less than 2 – remember it starts with a default value of zero

❏ Read through the Office records

❏ As each one is found, add 1 to the value of the Counter field

❏ Then display the Office number

❑ Check the value of the Counter field. If it is less than 2, loop back to read another Office record

❑ If it equals 2, stop the procedure.

ELSE

A procedural command that is used inside a conditional statement. Conditional statements first test a defined situation then act accordingly. Their command syntax consists of IF, ELSE and END commands.

Example:

Conditional statements know no boundaries. They exist in both the computer and real worlds. You run across them almost every minute of the day. Take for an example a situation where the office tea trolley has just arrived at your desk. Do you request a cup of coffee or tea?. Here's a situation that can only be resolved by using conditional statements.

If I fancy COFFEE then

    Buy a cup of Coffee

Else

    Buy a cup of Tea

End

If you like coffee then the first part of the conditional statement will be actioned, i.e. you'll purchase some coffee, otherwise the second part of the statement, that following the ELSE command is obeyed and a cup of tea is requested instead.

DataEase DQL code follows the same pattern:

```
For STAFF ;
   if SALARY < 15000 then
      modify records
         SALARY := SALARY + 2000
   else
      modify records
         SALARY := SALARY + 1000
   end
end
```

Here DataEase is commanded to process all the Staff records. If someone's current salary is less than £15,000 they are to be granted a £2,000 rise, ELSE they are only to receive a salary increase of £1,000.

END

A DQL procedural command that marks either the end of processing or the end of a section of processing. It is required to be used within any section of code that includes a FOR, CASE, IF or WHILE statement.

Usage: See Else DQL code above

ENTER A RECORD

This DQL processing command causes a record to be added to the specified form upon the database.

Example:

```
Enter a record in STAFF
   Copy all from data-entry
```

This code instructs DataEase first to create a record in the format of the Staff form. Then complete it with information taken from the DQL procedures data-entry screen.

EXIT

The EXIT command causes an action be immediately terminated. Processing then either continues back with the calling menu/procedure or with the next line of DQL code, if such exists outside the action just terminated.

Example:

```
For OFFICE ;
   list records
   OFFICE CODE in order.
   if OFFICE CODE = 11 then
      exit.
   end
end

For STAFF ;
   list records
   NAME in order.
end
```

The above code would cause Office records to be processed, their code number being reported, until an office with a code of 11 was reached. An Exit would be then be made from that processing and DataEase would start reading the Staff records instead. If the DQL code concerning Staff records was not present then an Exit from the procedure, back to a menu, would have occurred instead.

EXP
A Scientific Function that is used to calculate the exponential value of a numeric value.

Usage: EXPONENT := EXP (Field Name)

FIRSTC
This is a text function that returns a specified number of characters from the beginning of a string. Similar to the LEFT$ function in BASIC.

Usage: FIRST FIVE CHARACTERS := FIRSTC (Field Name,5)

If the value held with Field Name was Southend, the field First Five Characters would be given a value of South, these being the first five characters of that value.

FIRSTLAST
This text function switches around the first and last words contained within a string.

Usage: SWITCH := firstlast (Field Name)

If Field Name held a value of Turner Rose, the two words Turner and Rose would have their positions switched in order to provide the field named Switch with a value of Rose Turner.

FIRSTW
A text function that returns a specified number of words from the beginning of a string.

Usage: FIRST THREE WORDS := FIRSTW (Field Name,3)

Were the field Field Name to contain the wording Eat more Fish Today, the first three words of that string would be copied into the field First Three Words providing it with a value of Eat more Fish.

FLOOR
A mathematical function that rounds down a numeric value to the next integer.

Usage: NEXT INTEGER VALUE DOWN := FLOOR (Field Value)

A value of 3.99 would become 3.00 as would a value of 3.00

FOR

The most used DQL processing command. It specifies which forms records are to be processed.

Example:

```
For OFFICE ;
   List records
      OFFICE CODE code in order ;
      NAME .
end
```

DataEase would respond to the above DQL statements by reading all the Office records and displaying their information as each was processed.

FUTUREVALUE

This financial function will calculate the final value of a transaction once provided with its start value, the amount of each instalment, the interest rate and the number of payments to be made.

Usage: Total Amount := Futurevalue (start value, instalment amount, interest rate, no of payments)

GLOBAL

A keyword used within the definition of a variable that is going to be passed around between DQL procedures.

Usage: define GLOBAL "PARAMETER" String 10 .

This defines a variable named Parameter that is a string made up of 10 characters. The value held by this variable can be set/updated by any DQL procedure that contains the same variable definition and is controlled by a common Control procedure.

HIGHEST OF

This relational statistical operator locates the highest value for a specified field in a *related* form.

Example:

```
For OFFICE ;
   List records
      OFFICE CODE ;
      highest of STAFF STAFF RANK .
end
```

This DQL code instructs DataEase to read all the Office forms and report their office codes. In addition it is to find the highest value that is recorded inside the Rank field among all the Staff records associated with that office, and then display that value.

HOURS

A TIME function. It extracts the hour value from a time expressed in the 24 hour clock format.

Usage: HOUR := HOURS (Field Name)

If Field Name held a value of 22:34:20 then Hour would be given a value of 22.

IF

A DQL conditional command. See Chapter 5 for more information.

Usage:

IF condition THEN
action .
END

or:

IF condition THEN
action .
ELSE
action .
END

IF can also be used as a function that returns one of two specified values dependant upon whether a condition is *true* or *false*.

Usage: IF (condition, True value, False value)

where:

True value = The value to be displayed if the test condition is correct

False value = The value to be displayed if the test condition is not correct

Example:

```
For STORES ;
   List records
      BRANCH NAME in order ;
      NO OF STAFF ;
      IF (NO OF STAFF > 200, "Major Outlet", "Local Branch" )  .
end
```

A report resulting from the above DQL code could look like this:

Store	Staff Level	Status
Bolton	350	Major Outlet
Derby	220	Major Outlet
Leeds	400	Major Outlet
Mansfield	150	Local Branch
Nottingham	280	Major Outlet
Plymouth	120	Local Branch

IN

This is a Keyword. It's used to instruct DataEase to process a form, other than the query's current form, when executing the commands Enter a Record, Delete Records, Modify Records and List Records.

Example:

```
For STORE with PROFIT > 200000 ;
   modify records in STAFF
   BONUS = 500 .
end
```

This DQL instructs DataEase to read all the Store records searching for branches with a Profit of more than £200,000. When found, their related Staff records are to be modified such that their Bonus figures equal £500.

Note that it is the related record Staff that is being amended and NOT the current Store record.

IN ORDER

A command that tells DataEase to sort records into sequence and then display them in ascending order based upon the value held by a specified field(s).

Example:

```
For STORE ;
   list records
      PROFIT in order ;
      BRANCH NAME in order ;
      NO OF STAFF .
end
```

These DQL commands instruct DataEase to read all the Store records and display them in an order based upon the values held in the Profit and Branch Name fields. The Profit field's value takes priority over that of the Branch Name.

A report might appear like this:

Store Staff Profit

Store	Staff	Profit
Leicester	220	95000
Birmingham	250	100000
Exeter	180	100000
Gillingham	180	120000
Amersham	220	145000

IN REVERSE

A sorting operator that instructs DataEase to read records and display them in reverse order (e.g. Z to A) dependent upon the value held within a specified field(s).

Example:
```
For STORE ;
   list records
      PROFIT in reverse ;
      BRANCH NAME in reverse ;
      NO OF STAFF ..
end
```

These DQL commands instruct DataEase to read all the Store records and display them in an order based upon the values held in the Profit and Branch Name fields. The Profit field's value takes priority over that of the Branch Name.

A report might appear like this:

Store	Staff	Profit
Amersham	220	145000
Gillingham	180	120000
Exeter	180	100000
Birmingham	250	100000
Leicester	220	95000

INPUT

This DQL command echos all the facilities provided by record entry but allows the records to be processed before they are placed onto the database.

Example:

```
While Current Status not = 1 do
   input using ORDER BOOK into "TEMPRECORD" .

   case (Current Status)
      value 1 : break

      value 2 : Enter a record in ORDER BOOK
                Copy all from TEMPRECORD
                ORDER DATE := Current Date .
```

```
value 3 : Modify records in ORDER BOOK with
          ( ORDER NO = TEMPRECORD ORDER NO )
          ORDER STATUS := CONFIRMED    .

value 4 : delete records in ORDER BOOK with
          ( ORDER NO = TEMPRECORD ORDER NO )  .

   end

end
```

DataEase is instructed by this DQL to:

❑ Display the Order Book form as a data-entry screen. Record the information keyed into a temporary record named Temprecord.

❑ Every time the user presses a processing key, check the Current Status value – see Current.

<Esc> = sets Current Status value to 1

<F2 >= sets Current Status value to 2

<F8> = sets Current Status value to 3

<F7> = sets Current Status value to 4

If the value is 1 then quit the procedure – see Break

If the value = 2 (Save) record a new order upon the database based upon the information held within the temporary record.

If the value = 3 (Modify) then update the Order Book record that has the same reference number as that keyed into the temporary record, confirming the order.

If the record = 4 (Delete) then mark for deletion the Order Book record that has the same reference number as that keyed within the temporary record.

❑ Go back to the first step.

INSTALMENT

A financial function that calculates the instalment amount required for a financial transaction based upon the amount loaned, the deposit, interest rate and the number of payments.

Usage: instalment amount := installment (amount loaned, deposit, interest rate, number of payments)

Example:

```
instalment amount = instalment (12000,2000,10 / 12,120)
```

This example calculates a value of £166 for a loan of £12,000 with a £2,000 deposit over a 10 year period at 10% interest.

Note:

❏ The spacing around the interest rate figure 10 / 12 is important. The arrangement of a space before and after the slash sign must always be applied.

❏ The interest rate must be expressed in the same terms as the number of payments. As 120 refers to 10 * 12 months that must be reflected by the interest rate formula, monthly interest rates being 1/12th of the annual rate.

ITEM

This statistical operator orders DataEase to display extra specified information about a field, in addition to its value.

Example:

```
For PLAYERS ;
   List records ;
      NAME in order ;
         GOALS SCORED : item min max .
end
```

The report produced by this DQL could appear like this:

Player	Goals Scored
Andy Lake	5
Barry Stone	3
Charlie Deacon	7
Dave Kersley	2

Lowest No of Goals	2
Highest No of Goals	7

The Item property can also be used as a conditional statistical operator. This causes it to additionally provide Yes and No answers dependent upon whether or not the associated conditional statement is true or not.

Example:

```
For PLAYERS ;
   List records ;
      NAME in order ;
         GOALS SCORED : item min max ;
         GOALS SCORED > 3 : item .
end
```

The report produced by this DQL could then appear as this:

Player	Goals	Scored more than 3 goals
Andy Lake	5	YES
Barry Stone	3	NO
Charlie Deacon	7	YES
Dave Kersley	2	NO

Lowest No of Goals	2	
Highest No of Goals	7	

JOINTEXT

A function that combines two separate text values making one.

Usage: COMBINED FIELDS := JOINTEXT (Field Name 1, Field Name 2)

If Field Name 1 = *Quest* and Field Name 2 = *ion* then the field named Combined Fields would be provided with a value of *Question*.

JULIAN

A date function that's used to convert a date value into a Julian date. This is a five figure number in the format *yyddd* where *yy* = year number and *ddd* = the day's number within the year.

Usage: JULIAN DATE := JULIAN (Field Name)

If Field Name = *14/01/93* then Julian Date will have a value of 93014.

LASTC

A text function that returns a specified number of characters from the end of a string. Similar to the RIGHT$ function in BASIC.

Usage: LAST FOUR CHARACTERS := LASTC (Field Name,4)

If Field Name contained the value *PATRIOT* then the field named Last Four Characters would be set to *RIOT*.

LASTFIRST
This text function switches around the last and first words in a sentence.

Usage: SWITCH := lastfirst (Field Name)

If Field Name held a value of *Steven Thomas* then SWITCH would be allocated a value of *Thomas Steven*.

LASTW
This text function returns a specified number of words from the end of a sentence.

Usage: LAST THREE WORDS := LASTW (Field Name,3)

If Field Name holds a value of *Eat more Fish Today* then Last Three Words would contain a value of *more Fish Today*.

LENGTH
A text function that counts the numbers of characters held inside a string.

Usage: SIZE := LENGTH (Field Name)

Should Field Name contain a value of *Database* then SIZE will be given a value of 8.

LIST RECORDS
A DQL command that instructs DataEase to display the items listed for each record processed by the enquiry.

Example:

```
For PLAYERS ;
   List Records
      NAME ;
      POSITION ;
      AGE ;
      GOALS .
end
```

The above DQL code tells DataEase to read all the Players records and for each one display the contents of the Name, Position, Age and Goals fields in the report. Any other fields on the form will be ignored.

LOG
A scientific function that computes the natural base of a numeric value.

Usage: LOGARITHM := LOG (Field Name)

LOG10
This scientific function calculates the common base 10 of a numeric value.

Usage: LOGARITHM := LOG10 (Field Name)

LOWER
A text function that changes each character within a field into its lowercase equivalent.

Usage: lower case := LOWER (Field Name)

If Field Name holds a text value of *ToTTenhAM* then the field named lower case will be set to *tottenham*.

LOWEST OF
A relational statistical operator that finds the lowest value in a specified field upon a *related* form.

Example:

```
For STOCK ;
   list records
      STOCK ITEM in order ;
      lowest of ORDERS ORDERS TOTAL .
end
```

These DQL instructions tell DataEase to process all the Stock forms. As each one is read the value of the Stock Item field is to be reported plus the lowest value that was found within an Orders Total field upon the related Orders records.

The report might look like this:

Stock Item	Lowest Order
Blue Ties	1.50
Green Ties	1.20
Red Ties	2.00
White Ties	1.00

MAX
This statistical operator locates the highest value that's held within a specified field among all the records that are processed.

Example:

```
For ANGLERS with NO OF FISH > 0 ;
   list records
```

```
        NAME in order ;
        PEG ;
        NO OF FISH ;
        NO OF FISH : item max .
end
```

This DQL code could produce a report that looks like this:

Angler	Peg	No of Fish
Fred Flounder	14	1
Harry Halibut	12	6
Percy Plaice	10	5
William Whiting	11	3

Highest Catch 6

MEAN

A statistical operator. MEAN calculates the average value held within a specified field amongst all the records that are processed. This is calculated by adding all the values found for the field (including zero) together and then dividing that total by the number of records processed.

Example:

```
For ANGLERS ;
   list records
       NAME in order ;
       PEG ;
       NO OF FISH ;
       NO OF FISH : item mean .
end
```

This DQL code could produce a report that looks like this:

Angler	Peg	No of Fish
Colin Cod	13	0
Fred Flounder	14	1
Harry Halibut	12	6
Percy Plaice	10	5
William Whiting	11	3

Average Catch 3

MEAN OF

A statistical operator. MEAN OF calculates the average value held within a specified field amongst all the *related* records that are processed.

Example:

```
For MATCH ;
   list records
      LOCATION in order ;
      mean of ANGLERS ANGLERS NO OF FISH .
end
```

This DQL code instructs DataEase to read all the Match records. For each record read it is to display the value of the Location field and also the average value that was found within the No of Fish field upon its related Anglers records. The resulting report could appear as this:

Location	Average Catch
Chesil Beach	7
Dover Breakwater	10
Orford Island	8

MESSAGE

A DQL command that instructs DataEase to output a specified message upon the screen. It can be up to 255 characters in length and it is possible to control its display colouring and position.

Usage: message "message text" window pause .

The content of *message text* can be anything you wish, providing that you don't run to more than 255 characters of course. DataEase will automatically create a box or window upon the screen of sufficient size to display the message. You can divide the message up into several lines by inserting the vertical bar character I into your text in order to indicate where each line is to end.

If you wish to control the screen location of the message, the following parameters need to be inserted into the command, immediately before the message text.

Width	A number that describes how wide the box is to be
Start Line	The number of the line upon which the message is to start
Start	The number of the column within which the first character of the text is to appear.
No of Lines	The number of lines the message is to appear over

Window	The inclusion of this word tells DataEase to design a box within which to contain the message. Otherwise it will appear in the upper right hand corner of the screen and the length of your message will be restricted to just 40 characters.
pause	After a message has appeared upon the screen *within a window* DataEase will pause until the user presses a key to acknowledge the message. It will then clear the screen. If your message is not to be displayed within a window, the word *pause* will have to be included within your message instruction if your user is to have a realistic chance of reading the text.

Examples:

```
message "Invalid Student Number".
```

This is the most basic message instruction. DataEase will display the words *Invalid Student Number* in the top right-hand corner of the screen, and then continue processing without a pause. Your user will have to be a quick reader!

```
message "Invalid Student Number" pause .
```

Still a fairly basic message, again one that will appear at the top of the screen. However, this time the inclusion of the word *pause* instructs DataEase to await the user's acknowledgment of the message before it clears the screen.

```
message "ERROR - An invalid Student Number has been keyed" window .
```

A longer message has been possible this time because we've included the *window* command. This means that we are no longer restricted to just 40 characters and that the message will be displayed inside a box on the screen. DataEase will also now automatically await a response from the user. Therefore there is no need to include the *pause* command.

```
message "48,10,12,3, ERROR - |An invalid Student Number|has been keyed"
window .
```

This more elaborate instruction tells DataEase that we wish the message text to be displayed inside a box. The box is to be 48 characters wide and 3 lines deep. The top left-hand corner of the box is to be drawn at a position 10 lines down the screen and 12 columns in from its left hand side, the column numbers running from left to right across the screen.

It will appear on the screen as something like this:

```
ERROR –
An invalid Student Number
has been keyed
```

Colour controls can also be added to the text in a similar manner to the way they are included upon Data-entry screens, namely via the <F4> Hot Key method described in Chapter 3.

MIDC

A text function that returns a specified number of characters from the centre of a sentence. Similar to the MID$ function in BASIC.

Usage: MIDDLE CHARS = MIDC (Field Name,start position,no of characters)

Example:

```
MID THREE CHARS := MIDC (Field Name,5,3)
```

Assuming that Field Name has a value of *Handbook*, the field Mid Three Chars would be given a value of *Boo*. The fields value is built up thus: Locate the fifth character within the text – that positions us over the letter *B*. Then pick up the next three characters, inclusive of that character.

MIDW

A text function that returns a specified number of words from the centre of a sentence.

Usage: MIDDLE WORDS = MIDW (Field Name,start word number,no of words)

Example:

```
MIDDLE WORDS := MIDW (Field Name,2,3)
```

Given that Field Name = *Tropical aquarium fish swim in warm water*, the field named Middle Words would be provided with a value that reads *aquarium fish swim*. DataEase has identified the word *aquarium* as being the second word of the text, and then picked up the subsequent words *fish* and *swim* to bring the total number of words selected up to the required number of three.

MIN

A statistical operator that instructs DataEase to locate the lowest value that's held within a specified field among all the records processed.

Example:

```
For TEAMS ;
   List records
      TEAM NAME ;
      COLOURS ;
      POINTS ;
      POINTS : item min
end
```

The above DQL code tells DataEase to read all the Teams records, reporting each team's name, its colours and points total. In addition it is to search for the lowest number of points that have been awarded to any team. The resulting report could appear something like this:

Team	Colours	Points
Spread Eagle	Blue & White	25
Red Lion	Red & White	22
Three Crowns	Red & Bllack	29
The Prohibition	Green & Black	28

	Lowest Points	22

MINUTES

A time function that returns the minutes value from a time that's been set according to the 24 hour clock.

Usage: MINUTE VALUE := MINUTES (Field Name)

If Field Name contained a value of *09.27.35*, Minute Value would be set to 27.

MOD

A scientific function that calculates the remainder after one numeric value has been divided by another. If both values in the equation are integers then an integer remainder will be the result, otherwise a decimal value is returned.

Usage:

INTEGER VALUE = MOD (Field Name 1, Field Name 2)

If Field Name 1 = 6 and Field Name 2 = 4 then Integer Value would be set to 1.

DECIMAL VALUE = MOD (Field Name 1, Field Name 2)

If Field Name 1 = 6 and Field Name 2 = 2.5 then Decimal Value would be set to 2.4.

MODIFY RECORDS

This DQL commands instructs DataEase to apply amendments to a record that has already been stored upon the database.

Example:

```
For CUSTOMERS with PAYMENT RECEIVED = "YES" ;
   modify records
      ORDER CONFIRMED := "YES" .
end
```

This DQL tells DataEase to search for Customer records with a value of *Yes* in their Payment Received fields. It is then to amend the value of the Order Confirmed field contained upon those records to *Yes*.

MONTH

A date function that locates the month's value within a date.

Usage: MONTH NUMBER := MONTH (Field Name)

If Field Name has a value of *23/10/93*, Month Number will be set to 10.

NOT

A comparison operator that reverses the meaning of a test condition.

Example:

```
For STAFF with AGE not = 20
```

This DQL means select any Staff record where the Age field contains any value other than 20.

If multiple NOT statements are required, the word AND should be used rather than OR.

```
For STAFF with AGE = 20 or RANK = JUNIOR
```

This DQL statement would result in Staff records with either a value of 20 in their Age fields **OR** a value of *Junior* in their Rank fields being selected.

```
FOR STAFF with AGE not = 20 and RANK not = JUNIOR
```

The above statement instructs DataEase to only select those Staff records where the Age field is not equal to 20 **OR** the Rank field does not equal *Junior*. The word AND inside a NOT statement such as this works as if it was the word OR instead. Confusing isn't it?

OR

A logical operator that combines two test conditions.

Example:

```
For CAMERA with TYPE = SLR or LENS = 50 ;
   list records
```

This DQL statement instructs DataEase to find Camera records with either a value of *Slr* in their Type field or a value of 50 in their Lens field. If either field has the required setting, the record will be selected.

OTHERS

A keyword that is used inside a Case statement. It tells DataEase what to do with any values not caught by the preceding value conditions. It's a *catch all* type of command.

Example:

```
case (PORT)
   value "LIVERPOOL"
      assign temp PORT CODE := "LI" .
   value "DOVER"
      assign temp PORT CODE := "DV" .
   value "ABERDEEN"
      assign temp PORT CODE := "AB" .
   others :
      assign temp PORT CODE := "XX"
end
```

This DQL code instructs DataEase to look at the value of the Port field upon a record. If it is set to *Liverpool*, it is to provide the temporary field named Port Code with a value of *LI*. If it has a value of *Dover*, Port Code is to be set to *DV*; if *Aberdeen*, Port Code is to equal *AB*. If it's any other port the value of *XX* can be applied to the Port Code field.

PERCENT

A statistical operator that calculates the percentage of records that satisfy a specified test condition.

Example:

```
For CASSETTE;
   list records
      TITLE ;
      ARTIST ;
      MUSIC ;
      MUSIC = "Heavy Metal" : item percent .
end
```

DataEase is instructed by this DQL to read all the Cassette records, producing a report detailing their titles, the artist and music style. In addition it is to report the percentage of records processed that have a value of *Heavy Metal* inside their Music field. The report might appear like this:

Title	Artist	Music
Tropicana	Laby Dwight	Rock
Focum Point	The Patriots	Heavy Metal
Western Lights	Big John Tarry	Country & Western
Mosaic Patterns	Zilken Tribe	Heavy Metal

Heavy Metal Titles 50 %

PERIODS

A financial function that works out how long a financial arrangement needs to last in order for a target value to be realised, based on the current value, target value, instalment amount and interest rate being applied.

Usage: NO OF PERIODS := PERIODS (current value, target value, instalment, interest rate)

POWER

This scientific function raises a numeric value by the specified power.

Usage: RAISED VALUE := POWER (Field Name, exponent)

If Field Name had a value of 5, and the exponent was set to be 2 then Raised Value would be given a value of 25.

PRESENTVALUE

This financial function provides a means of calculating the initial loan amount that can be granted based on the loan period, the interest rate, target amount, and the repayment amount that has been budgeted.

Usage: AFFORDABLE LOAN := PRESENTVALUE (target amount,repayment amount, interest rate,loan period)

PROPER

A text function that converts the first letter in each word that is contained within a piece of text into its uppercase equivalent.

Usage: CONVERTED TEXT := PROPER (Field Name)

Should Field Name hold a value of *international rescue*, the field Converted Text would be given a value of *International Rescue.*

RANDOM
This math function calculates a random decimal value between 0 and 1.

Usage: DICE THROW := (RANDOM () * range) + lowest value

If an integer value is required within a certain range use this formula approach:

❏ Calculate the range within which you wish the random number to fall, i.e. a dice's range is usually between 1 and 6, therefore its range would be 6.

❏ Decide what the lowest possible value is to be – on our dice this would be 1

❏ Use this formula to calculate an integer inside the range required.

```
DICE THROW := (RANDOM () * 6 ) + 1
```

RATE
A financial function that calculates the required interest rate for a transaction once provided with the current value, target value, payment amount and number of payment periods.

Usage: INTEREST := RATE (Current Value, Target Value, Payment, Periods)

REORGANIZE
The command instructs DataEase to perform housekeeping actions on the designated form.

If a form has become inconsistent (an error message will inform you that this problem has occurred) it can be reorganised back into shape.

Alternatively, any records flagged for deletion will be actually removed from the database by this procedure.

Usage: REORGANIZE Form Name

Example:

```
REORGANIZE STUDENT
```

SECONDS
A time function that obtains the seconds value from a time expressed in the 24-hour format.

Usage: SECONDS IN TIME := SECONDS (Field Name)

If Field Name has a value of *11.30.25*, Seconds in Time will be set to 25.

SIN

A trigonometric function that calculates the sine of an angle. It expresses the answer in radians.

Usage: RADIANS := SIN (Field Name)

SINH

This trigonometric function calculates the hyperbolic sine of an angle expressing the result in radians.

Usage: RADIANS := SINH (Field Name)

SPELLCURRENCY

A spelling function that translates a numeric value into words.

Usage: WORDING := SPELLCURRENCY (Field Name)

If Field Name contained *25.50*, Wording would have a value of *Twenty Five pounds and 50 pence*. Note it is only the value before the decimal point that gets translated into words.

SPELLDATE

A spelling function that converts a date value into common form.

Usage: WORDING := SPELLDATE (Field Name)

Were Field Name to have a value of *12/08/93*, Wording would be set to *August 12, 1993*.

SPELLMONTH

A spell function that converts a numeric value into a month's name.

Usage: MONTH NAME := SPELLMONTH (Field Name)

Were Field Name to have a value of 5, Month Name would equal *May*.

SPELLNUMBER

This spell function converts the *integer* section of a number into a word.

Usage: INTEGER WORDING := SPELLNUMBER (Field Name)

If the value contained with Field Name is 9.25, Integer Wording would have a text value of *Nine*.

SPELLWEEKDAY

This spell function changes a numeric value into its corresponding day of the week. 1 meaning Monday and Sunday having a value of 7.

Usage: DAY OF WEEK := SPELLWEEKDAY (Field Name)

Should Field Name have a value of 3, Day of Week would be calculated as *Wednesday.*

SQRT

A scientific function that calculates the square root of a number.

Usage: SQUARE ROOT := SQRT (Field Name)

STD.DEV

A statistical Operator that calculates the standard deviation within a group of data.

Example:

```
For ORDERS with TOTAL > 1000 ;
   list records
      ORDER ID ;
      DATE ;
      CUSTOMER
      TOTAL : item std.dev .
end
```

STD.ERR

This statistical operator computes the standard error within a group of data.

Example:

```
For MOTORS with MILEAGE > 100000 ;
   list records
      CAR REGISTRATION ;
      MILEAGE : item std.err .
end
```

SUM

A statistical operator that adds together the values held within a specified field on the forms processed.

Example:

```
For MOTORS with VALUE > 5000
   list records
      CAR REGISTRATION ;
      MANUFACTURER ;
      VALUE : item sum .
```

The report would be as follows:

Car Registration	Manufacturer	Value
K234 2XR	Vauxhall	£7500
H521 74E	Ford	£7000
H765 45L	Fiat	£7200

	TOTAL VALUE	£21700

TAN

A trigonometric function that calculates the tangent of an angle, the result being expressed in Radians.

Usage: RADIANS := TAN (Field Name)

TANH

A trigonometric function that computes the hyperbolic tangent of an angle, the result being expressed in Radians.

Usage: RADIANS := TANH (Field Name)

TEXTPOS

This text function finds the position of some characters within a piece of text. Similar to the BASIC keyword INSTR$.

Usage: TEXT POSITION = TEXTPOS (Field Name, Text)

If Field Name holds a value of *Drink a cup of coffee* and the text to be found was *cup,* the field named Text Position would be given a value of 9.

TIMEAMPM

A time function that converts a time value presented in the 24-hour format into a 12-hour format with the appropriate AM or PM designation.

Usage: TWELVE HOUR TIME := TIMEAMPM (Field Name)

If Field Name was set to *14.53.22,* Twelve Hour Time would be provided with a value of 02.53.22 PM.

UPPER

A text function that translates characters within a bit of text into their uppercase equivalents.

Usage: HIGHER CASE := UPPER (Field Name)

If Field Name had a setting of *Muppet*, this instruction would result in the field named Higher Case being provided with a value of *MUPPET*.

VARIANCE

This statistical operator computes the average of the squared deviations from the mean within a set of data.

Example:

```
for STAFF with SALARY > 12000 ;
   list records
      NAME in order ;
      SALARY : item variance .
end
```

WEEKDAY

A date function that converts a date value into an integer that relates to the day number within the week, Monday being 1 and Sunday being 7.

Usage: DAY IN WEEK := WEEKDAY (Field Name)

If Field Name contained a value of *23/01/93*, Day in Week would equal 6, this day being Saturday.

WHILE

A DQL command that causes a series of actions to be performed while a specific test condition remains true.

Example:

```
define Temp "COUNTER" Number .

While temp COUNTER < 5 do
   For RECIPES with SERVE = "COLD" ;
      assign temp COUNTER := temp COUNTER + 1
      list records
         DISH ;
         PREPARATION TIME ;
         INGREDIENT .
   end
end
```

This DQL code first instructs DataEase to set up a temporary variable named Counter that has an initial value of zero. Then the WHILE command tells DataEase to list Recipes with a value of *Cold* in their Serve fields until COUNTER has a value of 5. This fields value is incremented as each such record is found and processed. Once a value of 5 has been realised, DataEase will exit from the DQL procedure.

YEAR

This date function calculates the year's number from a date field.

Usage: YEAR NUMBER := YEAR (Field Name)

If Field Name has a value of *01/10/93*, Year Number will be set to 93.

YEARDAY

This date function translates a date into the Julian day of the year.

Usage: JULIAN DAY NUMBER := YEARDAY (Field Name)

If Field Name holds a value of *05/02/93*, Julian Day Number will be given a value of 36, that being that date's day number within the year.

YEARWEEK

A date function that translates a date into the week number within the year.

Usage: WEEK NUMBER := YEARWEEK (Field Name)

Should Field Name have a value of *12/04/93*, Week Number will be set to 16, that being the number of the week within which that date appears.

INDEX

DQL commands are in UPPER CASE

Words for the wise - from
Sigma Press

Sigma publish what is probably the widest range of computer books from any independent UK publisher. And that's not just for the PC, but for many other popular micros – Atari, Amiga and Archimedes – and for software packages that are widely-used in the UK and Europe, including Timeworks, Deskpress, Sage, Money Manager and many more. We also publish a whole range of professional-level books for topics as far apart as IBM mainframes, UNIX, computer translation, manufacturing technology and networking.

A complete catalogue is available, but here are some of the highlights:

Amstrad PCW
The Complete Guide to LocoScript and Amstrad PCW Computers – Hughes – £12.95
LocoScripting People – Clayton and Clayton – £12.95
The PCW LOGO Manual – Robert Grant – £12.95
Picture Processing on the Amstrad PCW – Gilmore – £12.95
See also Programming section for *Mini Office*

Archimedes
A Beginner's Guide to WIMP Programming – Fox – £12.95
See also: *Desktop Publishing on the Archimedes* and *Archimedes Game Maker's Manual*

Artificial Intelligence
Build Your Own Expert System – Naylor – £11.95
Computational Linguistics – McEnery – £14.95
Introducing Neural Networks – Carling – £14.95

Beginners' Guides
Computing under Protest! – Croucher – **£12.95**
Alone with a PC – Bradley – £12.95
The New User's Mac Book – Wilson – £12.95
PC Computing for Absolute Beginners – Edwards – £12.95

DTP and Graphics
Designworks Companion – Whale – £14.95
Ventura to Quark XPress for the PC – Wilmore – £19.95
Timeworks Publisher Companion – Morrissey – £12.95
Timeworks for Windows Companion – Sinclair – £14.95
PagePlus Publisher Companion – Sinclair – £12.95
Express Publisher DTP Companion – Sinclair – £14.95
Amiga Real-Time 3D Graphics – Tyler – £14.95
Atari Real-Time 3D Graphics – Tyler – £12.95

European and US Software Packages
Mastering Money Manager PC – Sinclair – £12.95
Using Sage Sterling in Business – Woodford – £12.95
Mastering Masterfile PC – Sinclair – £12.95
All-in-One Business Computing (Mini Office Professional) – Hughes – £12.95

Game Making and Playing
PC Games Bible – Matthews and Rigby – £12.95
Archimedes Game Maker's Manual – Blunt – £14.95
Atari Game Maker's Manual – Hill – £14.95
Amiga Game Maker's Manual – Hill – £16.95
Adventure Gamer's Manual – Redrup – £12.95

General

Music and New Technology – Georghiades and Jacobs – £12.95
Getting the Best from your Amstrad Notepad – Wilson – £12.95
Computers and Chaos (Atari and Amiga editions) – Bessant – £12.95
Computers in Genealogy – Isaac – £12.95
Multimedia, CD-ROM and Compact Disc – Botto – £14.95
Advanced Manufacturing Technology – Zairi – £14.95

Networks

$25 Network User Guide – Sinclair – £12.95
Integrated Digital Networks – Lawton – £24.95
Novell Netware Companion – Croucher – £16.95

PC Operating Systems and Architecture

Working with Windows 3.1 – Sinclair – £16.95
Servicing and Supporting IBM PCs and Compatibles – Moss – £16.95
The DR DOS Book – Croucher – £16.95
MS-DOS Revealed – Last – £12.95
PC Architecture and Assembly Language – Kauler – £16.95
Programmer's Technical Reference – Williams – £19.95
MS-DOS File and Program Control – Sinclair – £12.95
Mastering DesqView – Sinclair – £12.95

Programming

C Applications Library – Pugh – £16.95
Starting MS-DOS Assembler – Sinclair – £12.95
Understanding Occam and the transputer – Ellison – £12.95
Programming in ANSI Standard C – Horsington – £14.95
Programming in Microsoft Visual Basic – Penfold – £16.95
For **LOGO**, *see Amstrad PCW*

UNIX and mainframes

UNIX – The Book – Banahan and Rutter – £11.95
UNIX – The Complete Guide – Manger – £19.95
RPG on the IBM AS/400 – Tomlinson – £24.95

HOW TO ORDER

Prices correct for 1993.
Order these books from your usual bookshop, or direct from:

SIGMA PRESS,
1 SOUTH OAK LANE,
WILMSLOW, CHESHIRE, SK9 6AR

PHONE: 0625 – 531035; FAX: 0625 – 536800

PLEASE ADD £1 TOWARDS POST AND PACKING FOR ONE BOOK.
POSTAGE IS FREE FOR TWO OR MORE BOOKS.
OVERSEAS ORDERS: please pay by credit card; we will add airmail postage at actual cost

CHEQUES SHOULD BE MADE PAYABLE TO **SIGMA PRESS.**

ACCESS AND VISA WELCOME – 24 HOUR ANSWERPHONE SERVICE.